Praise for

Yes, AI has many downsides, so we need to know what "wise use" means, and here is where Frontier's book is gold. Whether you're an AI enthusiast or a skeptic, *AI with Intention* challenges assumptions, offers fresh perspectives, and inspires meaningful dialogue about the future of education. AI is not good or bad; it is here to stay, and this is the best book I have read to introduce all to optimize the power of AI.

—**John Hattie,** laureate professor,
director of the Melbourne Education Research Institute

AI is transforming education, and intentionality is the key to ensuring it enhances, rather than diminishes, the human side of teaching and learning. *AI with Intention* is an essential guide for leaders and educators looking to understand and use AI to purposefully improve learning, teaching, and leadership in schools.

—**Catlin Tucker,** EdD, educator, author, and consultant

Educators can either resist AI or engage in meaningful conversations and take action to ensure it is used to positively impact teaching and learning. Growth requires adaptation. Schools must embrace change, and leaders must find ways to use AI to support teachers in personalizing instruction. In *AI with Intention,* Tony Frontier provides a thoughtful, practical guide to ensure leaders and teachers preserve the integrity of systems of effective teaching and learning while embracing the possibilities presented by AI.

—**Marc Cohen,** EdD, leadership coach,
The Leadership Link

AI with Intention is a must-have for every school leader and classroom teacher. To ensure meaningful learning, Tony Frontier clearly links guiding principles, strategic choices, and actionable steps. He provides the tools, strategies, and insights necessary to navigate the evolving landscape of AI in education with clarity and purpose.

—**Ruben Velarde Jr.,** EdD, learning innovator
and AI consultant

AI
WITH
INTENTION

Many ASCD members received
this book as a member benefit
upon its initial release.

Learn more at
www.ascd.org/memberbooks.

Understand
Empathize
Transform
Prioritize
Engage
Teach
Learn
Align
Lead

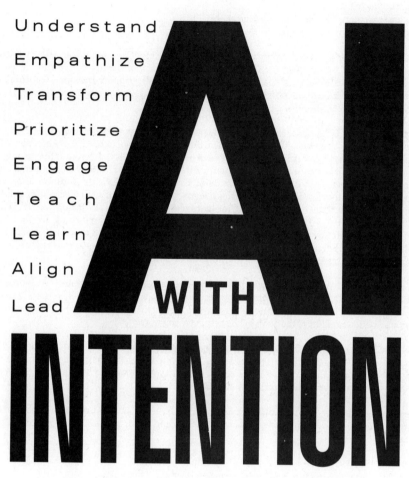

AI WITH INTENTION

Principles and Action Steps for Teachers and School Leaders

TONY FRONTIER

Foreword by Jay McTighe

Arlington, Virginia USA

2111 Wilson Boulevard, Suite 300 • Arlington, VA 22201 USA
Phone: 800-933-2723 or 703-578-9600
Website: www.ascd.org • Email: member@ascd.org
Author guidelines: www.ascd.org/write

Richard Culatta, *Chief Executive Officer;* Anthony Rebora, *Chief Content Officer;* Genny Ostertag, *Managing Director, Book Acquisitions & Editing;* Bill Varner, *Senior Acquisitions Editor;* Mary Beth Nielsen, *Director, Book Editing;* Megan Doyle, *Editor;* Lisa Hill, *Graphic Designer;* Cynthia Stock, *Typesetter;* Kelly Marshall, *Production Manager;* Shajuan Martin, *E-Publishing Specialist;* Christopher Logan, *Senior Production Specialist*

Select portions of Chapter 2 and Chapter 8 of this book are based on articles originally published by the author in *Educational Leadership* and have been expanded upon with additional details, examples, and research.

PAPERBACK ISBN: 978-1-4166-3362-4   ASCD product #124032
PDF E-BOOK ISBN: 978-1-4166-3363-1; see Books in Print for other formats.
Quantity discounts are available: email programteam@ascd.org or call 800-933-2723, ext. 5773, or 703-575-5773. For desk copies, go to www.ascd.org/deskcopy.

ASCD Member Book No. FY25-4 (May 2025 P). ASCD Member Books mail to Premium (P), Select (S), and Institutional Plus (I+) members on this schedule: Jan, PSI+; Feb, P; Apr, PSI+; May, P; Jul, PSI+; Aug, P; Sep, PSI+; Nov, PSI+; Dec, P. For current details on membership, see www.ascd.org/membership.

Library of Congress Cataloging-in-Publication Data
Names: Frontier, Tony author.
Title: AI with intention : principles and action steps for teachers and school leaders / Tony Frontier; Foreword by Jay McTighe.
Description: Arlington, Virginia : ASCD, [2025] | Includes bibliographical references and index.
Identifiers: LCCN 2025004829 | ISBN 9781416633624 paperback | ISBN 9781416633631 pdf | ISBN 9781416633648 epub
Subjects: LCSH: Artificial intelligence—Educational applications. | Educational technology. | Effective teaching. | Educational leadership.
Classification: LCC LB1028.43 .F78 2025 | DDC 371.33/463—dc23/eng/20250401
LC record available at https://lccn.loc.gov/2025004829

34 33 32 31 30 29 28 27 26 25   1 2 3 4 5 6 7 8 9 10 11 12

Foreword

Since ChatGPT 3.5 was first publicly released in November of 2022, I have been grappling with many questions, including *How can AI help teachers be more effective and efficient without undermining the development and refinement of their content and pedagogical expertise? In what ways can AI enhance student learning without short-changing their meaning making? How might we ensure that AI is used with integrity? How does AI fit within the present structure and cultures of schools? What systemic shifts will be necessary to fully realize the potential of this technology?*

AI with Intention offers a substantive and timely resource for any educator similarly wrestling with such questions. The book is organized into two parts to address its dual audiences of school leaders and classroom teachers. For leaders, Dr. Frontier highlights the critical distinction between first- and second-order change and makes the case for a transformational leadership approach to address the groundbreaking influences of AI in schools. He offers leaders a set of conceptually sound principles to guide their thinking as they make strategic decisions and take actions related to the opportunities and challenges of AI. Indeed, Frontier presents a virtual road map of key leadership actions, including helping the educational community understand the form and function of AI, posing thought-provoking questions challenging long-held assumptions about academic integrity, and clarifying expectations of how AI tools can be used in ways that ensure effective—rather than merely more efficient—teaching and learning.

In Part 2, Frontier focuses on how teachers and students can use AI tools to support deep and meaningful learning. First, he discusses the potential risks of AI to affirm students' misconceptions about learning and to impede teachers' efforts to design units and resources that are aligned to their students' learning needs. To address these challenges, he provides concrete action steps to take an empathetic approach to address students' perceptions of AI tools, emphasize a culture of learning, prompt AI tools with "the end in mind," and teach students how to use AI tools with agency to support active meaning making and authentic application of their learning.

Throughout the book, Frontier addresses the worrisome concern over students' use of AI tools to misrepresent their understanding and proficiency. Rather than focusing solely on finding ways to detect AI "cheating" and enacting disciplinary policies, he encourages educators to look below the surface to uncover the motivations for *why* students to want to use AI to shortcut their learning. He notes that when learning goals are clear and relevant, success criteria are made explicit, and students tackle authentic tasks with appropriate guidance, voice, and choice, then learners are more likely to be intrinsically inspired to put forth effort to learn rather than relying on AI to game the system and take the easy way out.

As I wrote this foreword, I found myself wondering how an AI tool might complete this task, and my curiosity got the best of me. I was surprised and impressed by the result; it generated the response in less than 30 seconds after digesting 154 pages of text. Yet it also left me quizzical, wondering whether a succinct summary of the book using many of the author's own words honors the spirit of a foreword when the purpose of any foreword is to invite and encourage readers to immerse themselves in an intellectually active process of making meaning from a text.

We can think of artificial intelligence as unleashing a torrent of white water into the societal river, and we are in a raft trying to stay afloat. Let Tony Frontier serve as our experienced river guide, helping us navigate the promises and pitfalls of this extraordinary and disruptive technology with intention—or as I like to say—by design!

Jay McTighe

Co-author of the *Understanding by Design*® series

Introduction

In his book *Here Comes Everybody,* Clay Shirky (2008) argued that "Communications tools don't get socially interesting until they get technologically boring" (p. 96). With the release of ChatGPT 3.5 in November 2022, generative artificial intelligence (AI) suddenly became technologically boring. Not only did this AI tool respond to conversational language and generate meaningful text, but no special programming language was necessary. All that was required was access to the internet.

In the months that followed, it became clear that students and educators found AI to be incredibly interesting. Students realized that these new AI tools were adept at answering homework questions or writing essays. Unsure of what these tools were capable of, administrators scrambled to block students' access. Articles with titles such as "The End of High School English" (Herman, 2022) and "I'm a Student. You Have No Idea How Much We're Using ChatGPT" (Terry, 2023) went viral. Some educators embraced the potential of AI tools to create efficiencies in teaching or to support students' learning. Others responded by modifying their school's or course's plagiarism policy by adding "including the use of AI" . . . and then went back to teaching as usual.

Since then, new AI models have been developed that further improve the capacity, accuracy, fluency, modality, and reliability of these tools. It is clear that these powerful tools will be everywhere all the time. Like smartphones and the internet, they will be ubiquitous.

While much of the initial hype and urgency around AI has settled, we're in the infancy of a new era. When transformative tools are suddenly available, there are always more questions than answers. But the questions we ask often reveal less about the transformative nature of the tools than of what we value in the existing system. For example, as I engage in dialogue with educators or look through social media posts in various AI for Teachers user groups, the two questions that I see and hear most often are some forms of the following:

- *Help! I'm drowning! Is there an AI tool that can … (create tests, quizzes, lesson plans, slide presentations, projects, rubrics; write letters of recommendation; score student writing; etc.)?*
- *Help! My students are using AI to do their … (homework, reading, writing, math, essays, research, projects, presentations, etc.)!*

These are important questions. When they are placed in sequence, the irony is obvious. Yet I don't think any hypocrisy should be inferred here. These questions speak to the fact that teachers *and* students are overwhelmed by the amount of information and the number of expectations they face every day. Both groups are looking for ways to use AI tools as *all* tools have been used in human history: to accomplish work of value more efficiently.

But just because a tool can be used to accomplish a task more efficiently does not mean is it more effective. When new tools are put to use, there are always benefits and costs. For example, the internet allowed information to be shared and accessed more easily. But the increased capacity has resulted in a world that is awash with low-quality information and clickbait (Carr, 2008; McQuade, 2024). Similarly, social media allowed more access to more social networks than at any time in human history. But feelings of isolation, loneliness, and stress are rampant (Haidt, 2024).

What will be the benefits and costs of AI tools when used for teaching or learning? To consider this question, let's start with three true statements.

- AI tools have the capacity to plan and accomplish almost any academic task.
- AI tools have nearly unlimited capacity to support effective teaching and learning.
- AI tools have nearly unlimited capacity to undermine effective teaching and learning.

Given the first claim, the line between the second and third claims has little to do with the capacity of AI tools. The costs and benefits of AI on teaching and learning will be determined by *how* AI tools are used.

Uses of AI tools that undermine effective teaching and learning look very different for teachers and students. For teachers, the risk is that their interactions with AI tools are too vague, resulting in lesson ideas, assessments, rubrics, or other instructional resources that are no better than what could have been found by randomly selecting the nth hit from a search engine or a teacher file-sharing site. For students, the risk is that their interactions with AI are too task-specific. Their superficial prompts are identical to the questions they've been assigned; they upload homework questions, math problems, or essays into an AI tool, and the tool spits out the answers.

These efficient but ineffective uses of AI tools run along parallel paths that eventually converge at the same place: students are either unable to or don't need to align and apply effort to strategies that result in deeper learning. Given this misalignment, the greatest threat AI poses to education may not be that students use AI tools to cheat, but that they receive answers from AI tools and think they've learned. Potentially even more debilitating, students come to see intelligence as something that is external, instantaneous, and effortless rather than something that is developed through a process that is internal, circuitous, and effortful.

How can we avoid these hazards and tap into the unlimited capacity of AI tools to support effective teaching and learning?

Intentional Teaching and Learning

The premise of this book is that the purpose of teaching is to create conditions where students are intrinsically motivated to apply effort to strategies that result in deeper learning. To do that effectively requires *intentional* action by both the teacher and the learner.

To act with *intention* is to consciously apply effort, in specific ways, to strategies and tools in order to attain a desired purpose or goal. Throughout this book, I use *intentional learning* and *intentional teaching* to mean the following:

- "Intentional learning refers to cognitive processes that have learning as a goal rather than an incidental outcome" (Bereiter & Scardamalia, 1989, p. 363).
- Intentional teaching refers to the alignment of "success criteria, feedback, learning strategies, teaching methods, activities, and assessments" (Hattie, 2023, p. 307) to support students' intentional learning.

Add the wisdom of those terms and definitions together, and a value statement to guide effective, intentional uses of AI tools comes into focus:

- To use AI with intention means teachers and students apply conscious effort, in specific ways, to AI tools to support intentional teaching and intentional learning.

The intent of this book is to move beyond conversations about what AI can or can't do and ask a deeper question: "What should *we* do, and what shouldn't *we* do to use AI tools to effectively support intentional teaching and intentional learning?" Whether you are a true believer who reaches for nearly every shiny AI-related object, a naysayer who sees AI as a dark cloud about to envelop us all, or an educator who feels powerless on all things AI because you aren't a technologist, you'll find ideas in this book that affirm and challenge your thinking and support your capacity to use AI tools more intentionally.

AI with Intention: How This Book Is Organized

Guiding principles are broad, strategic guidelines that inform decisions and actions to achieve goals. This book's chapters are organized around four guiding principles for leaders and four guiding principles for teachers. Each chapter explores a specific question aligned to that principle, a strategic choice educators can make to ensure intentional uses of AI tools, followed by aligned action steps.

In Chapters 1 through 4, I explain four guiding principles for school leaders to address the essential question: *How can leaders build capacity to ensure AI tools are used to effectively support intentional teaching and learning?* Figure I.1 shows the guiding principles, strategic choice, and aligned action steps.

In Chapters 5 through 8, I explain four guiding principles for teachers to address the essential question *How can teachers and students use AI tools to support intentional teaching and learning?* Figure I.2 shows the guiding principles, strategic choice, and aligned action steps.

While the two sections broadly focus on leading and teaching, both sections are relevant and will benefit all educators, regardless of their role.

FIGURE I.1 AI WITH INTENTION: GUIDING PRINCIPLES FOR SCHOOL LEADERS

Essential Question:		
How can leaders build capacity to ensure AI tools are used to effectively support intentional teaching and learning?		
Guiding Principle	**Strategic Choice**	**Action Steps**
Lead by Learning: Build a shared understanding of what AI is and isn't	Learning Organizations vs. Reactive Organizations	• Develop a basic understanding of the form and function of AI • Acknowledge misconceptions of AI • Identify patterns and trends in the development and use of AI • Learn the jargon of AI • Know the Gartner Hype Cycle
Take a Transformational Approach: Align leadership behaviors to the transformative implications of AI	Transformational Leadership vs. Transactional Leadership	• Align leadership behaviors to the magnitude of change • Ask big transformational questions • Place purpose and pedagogy before technology • Provide opportunities for low-stakes practice and play
Emphasize Integrity: Align expectations for academic integrity with intentional opportunities to learn	Humanism vs. Behaviorism	• Teach students what academic integrity is • Articulate expectations for stakeholders • Clarify the parameters of when and how AI tools can be used • Emphasize integrity, transparency, and explainability
Fidelity Before Efficiency: Empower educators to use AI tools to support intentional teaching and learning	Effectiveness vs. Efficiency or Automaticity	• Avoid the "twin sins" of AI integration • Discuss fidelity, efficiency, automaticity, and effectiveness • Take the expert approach: know *how*, *why*, and *when* • Ensure fidelity, transparency, and explainability

FIGURE I.2 AI WITH INTENTION: GUIDING PRINCIPLES FOR TEACHERS

Essential Question: How can teachers and students use AI tools to support intentional teaching and learning?		
Guiding Principle	**Strategic Choice**	**Action Steps**
Stand in Their Shoes: Take an empathetic approach to students' perceptions of AI tools and learning	Empathetic Design vs. Non-Empathetic Design	• Acknowledge students' misconceptions about learning • Acknowledge AI could deepen misconceptions about learning • Acknowledge misconceptions influence students' AI use • Take action to address student misconceptions • Affirm students' strengths, challenges, and interests • Take action to minimize cognitive load
Know Your Purpose: Prioritize students' strategies and efforts to learn	Learning vs. Compliance	• Acknowledge superficial uses of AI harm learning • Avoid the "twin sins" of curriculum design • Emphasize purpose for learning, not compliance • Teach students to plan, monitor, and self-assess • Emphasize integrity, transparency, and explainability
Prompt AI Tools Intentionally: Ensure AI tools are used to create clarity for teaching and learning	Clarity vs. Clutter	• Prioritize before prompting • Prompt with purpose • Revise for fidelity, document for transparency, and ensure explainability • Use AI as a fidelity coach • Use AI as an empathy coach
Use AI Tools for Intentional Learning: Empower students to use AI tools with agency	Independent vs. Dependent	• Pursue learning goals • Self-assess • Ask for help • Provide meaningful feedback • Be persistent and assertive • Apply strategies for intentional learning, including when using AI tools

Leadership and AI

Guiding Principles and Action Steps to Build Organizational Capacity to Ensure AI Tools Support Intentional Teaching and Learning

Lead by Learning
Build a Shared Understanding of What AI Is and Isn't

As computer scientist Jaron Lanier (2023) explains, "We're at the beginning of a new technological era—and the easiest way to mismanage a technology is to misunderstand it." By intentionally developing a shared understanding of what AI is and isn't, educators can make better-informed decisions about how to use AI tools to support intentional teaching and learning.

Learning Organizations vs. Reactive Organizations

Leaders of *learning* organizations know that in order to thrive, everyone on staff, regardless of position or seniority, must be committed to continuous learning (Senge, 2006). By contrast, leaders of *reactive* organizations assume that individuals should already have all the knowledge and skills necessary to be successful. If problems arise, they are attributed to unforeseeable external forces or as isolated issues.

In his seminal work on how leaders can help individuals and organizations navigate change, Peter Senge (2006) argues that the limiting factor of most organizations is not a lack of resources or effort, but a failure to learn:

> We all find comfort applying familiar solutions to problems, sticking to what we know best . . . pushing harder and harder on familiar solutions, while fundamental problems persist or worsen . . . what we often call the "what we need here is a bigger hammer" syndrome. But, the cure can be worse than the disease. Sometimes the easy or familiar solution is not only ineffective; sometimes it is dangerous. (Senge, p. 61)

According to Senge, when we don't get the results we desire, too often we shift the burden and blame onto others rather than reexamine our strategies. In schools, we shift the burden when we blame students, parents, or technology as the source of problems. The assumption is that we are doing the right work in the right way and that, for conditions to improve, others simply need to change their behavior. By absolving ourselves from responsibility, we disempower ourselves from taking effective action.

To lead a learning organization is to begin with the premise that we all need to continuously learn so we can be responsive to a world that is not static. In a learning organization, everyone is empowered to question assumptions, engage in meaningful dialogue, and adopt new ways of thinking. Staff in such organizations are well-positioned to successfully navigate both the challenges and opportunities of AI.

Action Steps: Lead by Learning

To build organizational capacity to understand how everywhere, all the time, access to generative AI tools could impact teaching and learning, follow these action steps:

1. Develop a basic understanding of the form and function of AI.
2. Acknowledge misconceptions about AI.
3. Identify trends and patterns in the use of AI tools.
4. Learn the jargon of AI.
5. Know the Gartner Hype Cycle.

Action Step 1: Develop a Basic Understanding of the Form and Function of AI

The "overnight" success of AI was the result of 80 years of work by mathematicians, linguists, and computer scientists (Mitchell, 2019). For most of that time, AI models that responded to and generated conversational language weren't reliable enough to be functional. In 2017, data scientists made a technical breakthrough (Vaswani et al., 2017) that allowed them to dramatically improve the capacity of AI models to interpret and generate understandable text.

Comparing an AI tool like ChatGPT to a more familiar technology like a search engine can be helpful in understanding how AI models work. The features of a search engine are built on a layer of computer code that uses a look-up-and-fetch approach to access content that has been labeled with keywords.

If a web page includes specific keywords, it will be presented in the list of links that the search engine yields. It is then up to the person doing the searching to go through the list and decide which links are most relevant.

Unlike a search engine, a large language model (LLM) such as ChatGPT doesn't use a look-up-and-fetch approach. Large language models are trained using deep learning, a type of AI that employs *transformers*—interconnected hierarchies of computer code—to detect patterns across thousands of layers of if-then scenarios. They've "learned" to do this by "observing" how words are grouped across millions of scanned books and huge amounts of internet data. The most powerful LLMs, like ChatGPT, have been *pre-trained* on so much data that they can make meaning of, and *generate,* conversational or "natural" language for nearly any purpose and in any format. Put these pieces together, and you can see where ChatGPT got its name; it is an example of a generative, pre-trained transformer that can chat using natural language.

So, how do these models generate meaningful language? The simplest explanation comes from mathematician Stephen Wolfram's (2023) book *What is ChatGPT Doing . . . and Why Does It Work?* His answer: "It's just adding one word at a time" (p. 1). Strip away the mathematical and linguistic complexity, and LLMs work by producing "a 'reasonable continuation' of whatever text it's got so far, whereby 'reasonable' we mean 'what one might expect someone to write after seeing what people have written on billions of webpages'" (p. 1).

Figure 1.1 lists some big ideas about the form and function of AI.

Action Step 2: Acknowledge Misconceptions About AI

There are endless misconceptions about AI. For some people, the term *artificial intelligence* brings to mind post-apocalyptic science fiction films; for others, it's a novelty tool that can be used to write silly poems about cats. Consider the following guidelines to move beyond misconceptions and support a more nuanced understanding of AI tools.

Don't Anthropomorphize Technology

If you've ever heard a student say something like "Well, that's what Google told me," you've been a witness to *anthropomorphism*: the attribution of human traits, emotions, or intentions to non-human entities. When we anthropomorphize technology, we deflect our attention from the actions and intentions of

FIGURE 1.1 THE FORM AND FUNCTION OF AI

- AI models consist of layers of code and mathematical algorithms that determine or predict probabilities of what word (or pixel) is most likely to come next in a sequence.
- Because AI models are trained on existing data, biases or inaccuracies in the training data will be reflected in the tools' output.
- AI models "hallucinate"—that is, they may generate output that is detached from reality.
- AI models are comprised of "black box" algorithms, the inner workings of which are so complex that it is nearly impossible to explain precisely why the tools generate the responses they do.
- The output of AI tools is only as strong as the input the user provides through prompts.

the people using the technology. The student who says Google "told" them something is omitting the fact that they were responsible for typing a specifically worded question into Google and selecting a particular search result. Anthropomorphism is a shortcut for clear thinking.

Because AI tools can engage in dialogue and use colloquial language, it can be a challenge not to anthropomorphize them. As I've written this book, I've caught myself writing that AI can *read, write, explain, understand,* and *decide* things, to cite just a few examples. But AI should never be described as a thinking, living thing. Educators can help students think more clearly about the form and function of AI tools by using precise language that accentuates the user's role in providing prompts and checking, modifying, augmenting, revising, or ignoring the tool's output.

Don't Think of AI as a Monolith

Artificial intelligence isn't a single thing (Hunter, 2023). The term refers to a broad range of technologies and models that have been developed by hundreds of researchers and are being used in thousands of different ways by millions of different people. Saying AI is "good" or "bad" is a bit like saying books are "good" or "bad."

One way to avoid talking about AI as a monolith is to clarify if you are talking about "AI," an "AI model," or an "AI tool." Use the term *AI* in isolation if you are talking about it as a broad field of data science. Specify that you are talking about an *AI model* if you are describing the behind-the-scenes features of a specific large language model. Finally, specify that you are talking about an *AI tool* if you are describing the interface the user sees and interacts with on their computer screen.

By using precise language to talk about AI, we can avoid sweeping generalizations and ask specific questions that allow for important conversations about the application of *specific* AI models and tools. For example: *What AI model is being discussed? How was this AI model or tool designed to be used? How might this specific AI tool be used to benefit teachers and learners? How might this AI tool be problematic for teachers and learners?* Knowing the answers to these questions allows us to engage in more reasoned conversations with colleagues, students, parents, board members, and vendors about the form and function of AI.

Avoid Automation Bias

In 2012, a group of tourists visiting Australia drove their car into the ocean. Their GPS app was blissfully unaware (yes, I just anthropomorphized) that the road they were told to take had been submerged in a tidal event (Fujita, 2012). These tourists were victims of automation bias: our propensity to put faith in technology even when it is clearly wrong. If the tourists had asked a local for directions and he'd replied, "Just take the road into the ocean, drive through the water for about a mile, and turn right," they certainly wouldn't have taken his advice.

There is something magical about LLMs. When that cursor blinks for a few seconds and then generates a sensible response at 100-plus words a minute, it appears to demonstrate a level of command and fluency in the topic or task that must transcend that of humans. Be skeptical. Yes, AI models can accurately sift through mountains of data and generate meaningful—even insightful— responses. But they aren't omniscient, and their output can include errors and "hallucinations" in the form of falsehoods and mistakes. No matter how "magical" a technology tool may appear to be, its output should always be subject to fact-checking, verification, and common sense.

Action Step 3: Identify Trends and Patterns in the Development and Use of AI Tools

By identifying trends and patterns in the development and use of AI tools, individuals and organizations will be better positioned to proactively anticipate, and address, opportunities, challenges, and needs.

Patterns and Trends Related to Access and Use of AI Tools

- **AI tools that are responsive to natural language will be ubiquitous.** Search engines, word-processing programs, and other applications will be equipped with increasingly sophisticated personal assistants, writing coaches, math tutors, and more.

- **Multimodal AI tools will be ubiquitous.** AI tools that can make images or videos based on text prompts, generate text that explains an image, or narrate what is happening in a video will become increasingly sophisticated and accurate.

- **AI tools will be inaccurate and unreliable.** AI models and tools make mistakes. When you hear an anecdote about—or experience—faulty AI output, ask yourself if it was due to a limitation of the tool itself, a misapplication of the tool for its intended purpose, or operator error.

- **AI tools are becoming increasingly capable, accurate, and reliable.** According to Andrew Ng (2023) of Stanford University, whereas it used to take nearly a year to develop robust AI models based on large volumes of data, it now takes less than a week. The lesson? If you see an AI tool produce clunky, error-laden output, don't think to yourself, "AI will never be able to do this right." Instead, think to yourself, "Data scientists are working on that. I should revisit this in a few months to see what progress has been made."

- **AI models will vary in capability, functionality, and cost.** The answer to the question "What is the best AI model to use?" depends on what you want to do with it, how often you will use it each day, and how much you are willing to pay. Free generative AI tools are already embedded in many apps and products from Microsoft, Google, Apple, and Adobe. But the most powerful, reliable, and flexible generative AI models (such as Claude, Gemini, and ChatGPT) typically cost about $20 per month. To navigate this ever-changing landscape, Wharton's Ethan Mollick (2025) provides an ongoing, insightful, and easy-to-understand analysis of the features, benefits, and drawbacks of the leading models on his blog.

- **AI is a profit-driven industry.** Companies have invested billions of dollars in AI tools in just the last few years (Bass, 2023), with the ultimate goal of achieving a return on that investment. Remember, it is the job of AI companies to ask, "How could this tool be used to make profits?" And it is our job as educators to ask, "But how does that support intentional teaching and learning?" Just because a tool has the capacity to accomplish a task doesn't mean that task is important or the output will be effective.

- **AI is creating ethical, legal, and policy challenges.** Access to AI tools is blurring legal and ethical lines related to intellectual property, privacy, safety, and personal responsibility among individuals, within organizations, and across communities. However, don't expect any laws or lawsuits to end the development of AI tools; the AI genie can't be put back in the bottle. Some guardrails may be put in place, but educators will need to be continuously aware of the challenges that can arise from students' and staffs' use—or misuse—of AI tools.

- **The effectiveness and utility of an AI tool depends largely on the user.** Tools are effective when they are in the hands of a skilled user who knows how to accomplish the task for which the tool has been designed. As Oguz Acar (2023) argues, as AI tools become more powerful and easy to use, the user's ability to frame problems and tasks in meaningful ways and to properly understand a tool's output is vital. Without a clear purpose and a clear understanding of the real-world context in which the AI tool is being applied on the part of the user, Acar argues, "even the most sophisticated prompts will fall short."

- **Prompting AI tools has more to do with domain expertise than technological expertise.** While there are some general principles that need to be utilized to prompt AI tools effectively, no knowledge of computer programming language is required. If a science teacher is using an AI tool to plan a unit, it is the teacher's expertise in her content and her expertise in curriculum design that will allow her to apply the language and knowledge necessary to interact with the tool effectively.

Challenges and Opportunities Related to Schools, Students, and Learning

- **Students of all ages will be increasingly likely to cross paths with AI tools.** Generative AI tools will be ubiquitous. While there are age restrictions on direct use of AI models and tools today (typically 13+ with parental consent), even students below age 13 will be increasingly likely to interact with AI tools. This is because more and more apps and websites embed generative AI models to run behind the scenes—with guardrails for content moderation and privacy in place—so they can be used by students. However, as we know, kids find their way onto apps regardless of age restrictions. This doesn't mean we should condone that behavior. Just because an app is age-restricted or blocked at school, doesn't mean students aren't using them on their phones or at home. Administrators and teachers need to be vigilant to ensure students are not being assigned tasks, or cannot access websites at school, that violate user agreements, local policies, or federal guidelines.

- **AI tools have the potential to minimize existing opportunity gaps.** AI tools are remarkably adept at modifying and augmenting learning resources and teaching tools for differentiated instruction. They are also increasingly effective as tutoring resources across subject areas. American families spent $2.49 billion on private tutors in 2021 (Annenberg Institute at Brown University, 2022); not surprisingly, much of this money was spent by families that could afford to do so. Thanks to AI, it's possible that any student with an internet connection can access an endlessly patient, well-informed tutor with the ability to explain or assist with content in a way that matches their precise level of need.

- **AI tools have the potential to create new, or deepen existing, opportunity gaps.** AI tools are only useful to students if they can access them. Not all students have internet access or even a computer at home. Furthermore, a recent study of over 4,500 students found that even when students were given access to online tutoring, only 19 percent took advantage of it (Robinson et al., 2021). Even more disconcerting, students who were struggling in their coursework were less likely to access the resource than their higher-achieving peers. Educators must work to ensure that AI tools don't simply become another resource for the advantaged.

- **Access to AI tools will create new challenges for teachers to make reliable inferences about student learning.** The word *assessment* derives from the Latin *assidere*, meaning to "sit beside or with." Some of the strongest research on student learning emphasizes the power of classroom assessment for helping teachers and learners work together to prioritize their efforts to teach and learn. At the center of this partnership is the ability of teachers to discern what students can and cannot do independently. When students use AI tools, it's harder for educators to do this reliably. This will require teachers to rethink how to assess students in ways that ensure the integrity of students' evidence of learning, a topic that will be discussed in detail in this book.

- **AI tools will create new challenges for educators to support students' social-emotional needs.** In 2023, the U.S. surgeon general issued an advisory on social media and youth mental health (Office of the Surgeon General, 2023). This report cites a range of studies pointing to an increased risks of depression, bullying, anxiety, negative body image, and lower self-confidence among adolescents who spend more than three hours a day on social media.

It is all too easy to see how AI could exacerbate these challenges. We have already seen deepfakes used to disparage or embarrass both students and educators. How should schools respond when students are bullied by AI bots or turn away from human friendships in favor of AI-generated avatars? These new realities impact our students' social-emotional well-being and we must be prepared to confront them.

Action Step 4: Learn the Jargon of AI

According to Robert Marzano and colleagues (2011), a shared language of professional practice is an essential element of systems that collaborate effectively. It is easy to forget that when the internet was first widely accessible to schools a generation ago, most people had to learn terms such as *browser*, *search engine*, and *domain* so they could engage in rational discussions with colleagues about policies, purchases, and effective practice.

Following are some straightforward definitions of basic AI terms that can make discussions about this technology more accessible to teachers, administrators, and school board members:

- **Agent:** An AI tool that is automated to run an entire set of actions and processes with just a single initial prompt.
- **Alignment:** The process of ensuring that the goals of AI models and tools agree with human ethics and values. (Brian Christian's 2020 book *The Alignment Problem: Machine Learning and Human Values* provides a deep dive on this topic.)
- **Application programming interface (API):** A tool that allows two different applications to talk to each other. For example, a start-up AI education company can acquire an API key, or passcode, that allows it to run another company's LLM, such as ChatGPT or Claude, behind the scenes.
- **Bias:** An assumption made by an AI model based on skewed training data.
- **Compute:** The amount of processing power, memory, and storage necessary for a computer or computer network to meet the complex demands of generative AI tools.
- **Constitutional AI:** A set of parameters related to ethics, appropriateness, or safety that articulates what an AI model will or will not do; a separate model checks to ensure the parameters are followed before output is produced.
- **Deep learning:** A function of AI that imitates the human brain by using differently weighted layers of code and algorithms to identify, discern,

apply, and generate complex patterns. Unlike machine learning, which requires pre-labeled data, deep learning "discovers" useful patterns derived from set parameters and then develops and refines the weights assigned to each layer.

- **Emergence:** The presence of complex behaviors in an AI model based on only a few simple rules or parameters.
- **Explainability:** The extent to which an AI model can justify and explain its results or outputs in a manner that can be understood by the user.
- **Foundational (or frontier) model:** A large AI model trained on massive amounts of data that can be used to perform a variety of text, image, audio, or video-related tasks beyond its initial training. These models can serve as the starting point for models that are designed to more efficiently accomplish more specific tasks. Examples include Claude, Gemini, and ChatGPT.
- **Generative AI:** AI tools that have been designed to respond to prompts by generating new and original content in the form of words, images, video, or music based on patterns that have been learned based on examples on which the underlying model has been trained.
- **Hallucination:** AI-generated responses that are inaccurate or wildly at odds with reality.
- **Interpretability:** The degree to which the internal processes of an AI model can be explained or understood by humans.
- **Large language model (LLM):** A foundational AI model that has been trained on massive amounts of data to make meaning of and generate meaningful passages of natural language text. LLMs can also be used to shift among modalities (e.g., text to image, image to text).
- **Machine learning:** An approach to AI whereby a model learns from and accomplishes tasks based on pre-labeled data through patterns of reinforcement and then applies what it has learned to un-labeled training data.
- **Narrow AI:** AI models trained in a specialized skill set to focus on specific tasks.
- **Neural network:** Underlying networks of AI models that are built on layers of differently weighted lines of code called *neurons*. These networks are modeled on neurologists' understanding of how the human brain processes information.
- **Natural language generation (NLG):** The capacity of an AI tool to generate data as intelligible, meaningful text that can be understood by humans.

- **Natural language processing (NLP):** The capacity of an AI tool to receive and make meaning of patterns in data that have been entered as written text or spoken words.
- **Natural language understanding (NLU):** The capacity of an AI tool to make nuanced meaning of data that has been entered as written text or spoken words by accurately interpreting implicit meaning or accurately ignoring grammatical errors or typos.
- **Overfitting:** What happens when a predictive model is not trained on enough data, resulting in errors when the model is applied to new data.
- **Parameters:** The internal variables and associated weights and biases that an AI model develops from training data and then applies to generate appropriate responses.
- **Prompt:** A query or command provided to an AI tool as the basis for its response.
- **Prompt engineering:** The process of giving commands to or asking questions of an AI tool in a manner that maximizes efficiency and fidelity of the AI model's response to the user's intentions or needs.
- **Reinforcement learning:** A type of machine learning whereby an AI model self-adjusts through trial and error and human input to become more accurate.
- **Supervised learning:** A type of machine learning whereby an AI model receives accurately labeled training data through which it "learns" to recognize, sort, or generate accurate responses based on salient features.
- **Token:** A unit of text that can be recognized by an AI model. Because AI models cannot make meaning of language the way humans can, letters, words, and parts of words are given pre-assigned numerical values.

Action Step 5: Know the Gartner Hype Cycle

The history of technology is littered with both spectacular breakthroughs and catastrophic failures. While it is often impossible to predict which specific innovations and associated products will succeed or fail, we *can* predict how people will respond to innovations. The Gartner Hype Cycle (Gartner, 2024) provides a concrete framework for taking a measured response to innovation. The cycle begins with an innovation trigger, followed by a peak of inflated expectations, disillusionment, more enlightened and realistic expectations, a plateau of productivity, and, eventually, a new triggering event.

Using the Hype Cycle as a narrative structure, the recent response to breakthroughs in AI could be explained as follows:

In November of 2022, technology-related social media and news services reported extensively on the *triggering event* of the release of ChatGPT 3.5. By the beginning of 2023, ChatGPT was being discussed in traditional media and casual conversation as either the "end of poverty" or the "end of the world." When a technology has permeated this deeply into the collective culture, it is on a path toward a *peak of inflated expectations*. AI-related products flooded the market, and consumers were eager to try them. But many of these products failed to deliver on their promises or left users frustrated and in a state of *disillusionment*. During the disillusionment phase, there is a collective acceptance of the limitations of the technology. This leads to a *slope of enlightenment* where more realistic expectations, new approaches, and the development of the next iteration of products occur. Eventually, expectations, capacity, and strategy will align and lead to a *plateau of productivity*. Then the process will start all over when the next game-changing breakthrough becomes the new *triggering event*.

When you as an educator are presented with a technology in the early phases of the Gartner Hype Cycle, it is wise to be curious about the technology but skeptical about the tools. To be curious means you ask many pointed questions. To be skeptical means you challenge assumptions and seek facts to discern the gaps between what is possible, what is effective, and what is deliverable. Examples of questions you could ask to discern these gaps include the following:

- Does a fully functional product exist, or is this a vision of what is intended?
- Does this tool exist because it addresses an important need or simply because AI has the capacity to accomplish these tasks?
- What are some examples of challenges and opportunities that classroom teachers have experienced when using this AI tool?
- What are the potential benefits and drawbacks of using an AI tool to complete this task rather than a human?
- Are any educators or students in my organization already using similar AI tools? If so, what have they learned?

When a new innovation comes along, it can be tempting to go all in . . . or to pretend it doesn't exist. Effective leaders will acknowledge the limitations of either-or dichotomies and think more systematically about the realities that lay ahead.

If you find yourself chasing every AI-related shiny object that comes along, know that there are opportunity costs in terms of wasted fiscal resources, initiative fatigue, and not knowing whether the newly acquired tools can be used to actually support more intentional teaching and learning. Be patient with school or systemwide investments. Find a balance between building systems-level capacity to learn about the new tools while leaving some space to learn from others' disillusionment.

Or, if you find yourself taking a "wait and see" approach to let the AI space settle down a bit before formally establishing direction and strategy, you've marked your calendar for a day that will never come. Teachers (and students) are already putting AI tools to use because they are easily accessible. They can benefit from intentional opportunities to learn how to use these tools effectively.

In a learning organization, leaders play an important role in building the capacity of others to navigate change. That charge can feel overwhelming and ambiguous. The Gartner Hype Cycle is an example of a framework that can be used to lead others along predictable portions of a more manageable series of paths.

Questions for Reflection and Discussion

1. What are the characteristics of a learning organization versus a reactive organization? Why is it important to respond to AI tools as a learning organization rather than a reactive one?

2. What are some important things to know about how LLMs work?

3. Why is it important to address misconceptions about AI? How should we talk about AI tools with students and other educators?

4. What are some trends in the development and use of AI tools? What are some possible implications of these trends for society in general? What about for schools, teachers, and learners?

5. How can a shared understanding of the language of AI support effective collaboration and dialogue with colleagues?

6. What is the Gartner Hype Cycle? How can understanding the cycle support making effective decisions when presented with new AI tools?

7. How can some of the ideas in this chapter help you to use AI tools in a manner that supports rather than undermines effective teaching and learning?

2

Take a Transformational Approach
Align Leadership Behaviors to the Transformative Implications of AI

Effective leaders apply different strategies to different types of challenges. Sometimes, they need to hold others accountable to follow existing norms and routines. Other times, they need to support efforts to navigate incremental change; a new initiative needs to be implemented, and staff members need to learn some new procedures and strategies to make that happen. But sometimes a change occurs that is so significant, the assumptions about how the system is supposed to work are no longer relevant. Strategies and approaches that had worked in the past have little or no impact. In fact, applying those strategies may be making matters worse. How can leaders help others effectively navigate change as transformative as ubiquitous access to AI tools when there are so many variables and so many unknowns?

First- and Second-Order Change

Effective leaders provide stability to their organizations. One way they do this is by *managing the status quo*. Here, routine strategies are applied to routine tasks to ensure the buses arrive on time, instructional materials are available, and there is a teacher in every classroom. But maintaining order is not enough to ensure organizational effectiveness. Leaders also need to help others navigate change.

The term *magnitude of change* is used in leadership theory to describe the complexity of change faced by an organization. First-order change is gradual; existing knowledge, skills, and strategies can be applied to navigate the change successfully. Examples of first-order change could include moving from an eight-period day to a seven-period day or implementing a different electronic gradebook.

Second-order change is seismic. It is preceded by a triggering event that involves a "dramatic departure from the expected that alters the system in fundamental ways . . . requiring new ways of thinking and acting" (Marzano et al., 2005, p. 66). The triggering event could be internal, such as a strategic shift from a traditional grading system to a standards-based system of assessment and grading. Or the triggering event could be external, such as a global pandemic or sudden access to AI tools.

Transactional vs. Transformational Leadership

As leaders work to help others navigate change, they need to make decisions about how to align their leadership behaviors to best meet the needs of those they serve. Transactional approaches to leadership emphasize the pursuit of outcomes or goals in exchange for rewards, recognition, or compensation (Burns, 1978). The core assumption of a transactional approach to leadership is that outcomes can be improved by creating incentives to help others apply existing skills more frequently, modifying one's strategies, or using new tools.

On the other hand, the fundamental assumption of a transformational approach to leadership is that individuals must be both challenged and supported to think differently about the very nature of the work they are expected to engage in. Transformational approaches to leadership emphasize the importance of individual consideration, intellectual stimulation, inspirational motivation, and idealized influence (Bass, 1985). This requires leaders to engage in behaviors that acknowledge individuals' perceptions, challenge and stimulate their thinking, motivate them to pursue challenging goals, and model the openness and effort required to succeed.

Effective leaders intentionally align their strategies and behaviors to support others' efforts to manage the status quo or navigate change (Figure 2.1). Many of the challenges related to the second-order challenges brought about by access to AI can be best supported by a transformational approach to leadership.

FIGURE 2.1 THREE RESPONSES TO CHANGE

	Status Quo Management	Transactional Response	Transformational Response
Premise	Current skills and outcomes are acceptable.	Current outcomes should be improved by applying existing skills more frequently, with different incentives, or to different tools.	New ways of thinking about the nature of their work, how they serve others, and what strategies they use are necessary to adapt to external innovations and improve outcomes.
Knowledge	Apply current knowledge and beliefs.	Add to current knowledge but maintain existing beliefs.	Knowledge that had worked well in the past may no longer be adequate or relevant; new beliefs or ways of thinking are necessary.
Strategies	Apply existing strategies to routine tasks.	Apply existing strategies to new tools or with more frequency.	Strategies that had worked well in the past may no longer be adequate or relevant; new strategies are necessary.
Aligned Leadership Behaviors	• Manage logistics • Maintain current strategies • Follow and enforce existing procedures and roles or create new policies to stifle innovation	• Maintain beliefs • Integrate new resources • Offer answers and solutions • Clarify rules or modify procedures and policies • Create new incentives and/or consequences	• Begin with mission, vision, and purpose • Challenge assumptions and existing mental models • Engage teams in dialogue around big, open-ended questions • Create opportunities for others to explore and learn new ideas, skills, and strategies • Align new mental models to new beliefs, skills, and strategies
Risks of Misaligned Leadership to Second Order Change	External forces that required attention are stifled, ignored or missed, resulting in declining or irrelevant outcomes.	Transformational challenges are treated like transactional problems, resulting in increased effort, new incentives, and/or acquisition and use of new resources but stagnant or declining outcomes.	Stakeholders may resist changes because they don't understand the need for new ways of thinking, or leaders may mistakenly assume others understand the need for a transformational response to the change, but believe they are merely too stubborn or incompetent to change.

Source: Adapted from information in *Five Levers to Improve Learning* by Tony Frontier and James Rickabaugh, 2014, ASCD.

None of these magnitudes of change is "better" or "worse" than another; different situations require different leadership strategies. To draw on the ideas of Heifetz and Linsky (2002), the greatest mistake leaders make is treating a transformational challenge as though it is a transactional problem. By considering the distinctions among status quo management, transactional change, and transformational change (see Figure 2.1), leaders can more mindfully help others navigate the transformational challenges and opportunities related to ubiquitous access to AI tools.

Action Steps: Take a Transformational Approach

To provide the leadership necessary to navigate the changes brought about by ubiquitous access to powerful AI tools, consider the following action steps:

1. Align leadership behaviors to the magnitude of change.
2. Ask big, transformational questions.
3. Place purpose and pedagogy before technology.
4. Provide opportunities for low-stakes practice and play.

Action Step 1: Align Leadership Behaviors to the Magnitude of Change

To understand the importance of aligning leadership behaviors to the intended magnitude of change, consider the following.

Status Quo Response

Trying to maintain the status quo in the face of second-order change can be counterproductive. For example, given the unknowns of ChatGPT 3.5 upon its release, many schools simply blocked access in order to manage risks and maintain the status quo. However, this is not a long-term solution to the challenges posed by students' access to AI tools. Blocking local access to something that's widely available could increase the digital divide, since students with access to these tools outside school will still be able to use them. Another ineffective approach to try to maintain the status quo is to simply pretend the innovation doesn't exist. But this ignores the reality that students may be using AI tools in ways that harm their learning, and they won't have any opportunities to learn how to use the tools effectively or responsibly.

Transactional Approaches to AI at the School Level

A transactional approach to second-order change can also be problematic. When a new innovation becomes accessible, users typically apply their existing assumptions, knowledge, and strategies to the tool or resources to accomplish a task more efficiently. For example, shortly after the release of ChatGPT 3.5, many users' first instinct was to use it as a next-generation search engine. This transactional approach—I give the tool a search command and the tool gives me the information I want—has been ingrained in our mental model of how the internet works. But since ChatGPT 3.5 was not designed to be used as a search engine, it left many users disappointed and confused about all the hype.

Some examples of transactional responses to AI tools at the school or district level could include the following:

- Modifying policies by simply adding the words "artificial intelligence" or adding consequences to deter misuse.
- Approving professional learning goals related to "using AI tools more frequently" without support or guidance related to how they should be used effectively.
- Acquiring a variety of AI tools without a broader strategy for how, when, and why to use them.

These approaches are transactional because they rely on consequences, incentives, or acquisition to achieve goals. These surface-level approaches are unlikely to build the capacity of individuals to adapt in ways that help them successfully navigate second-order change.

Transactional Approaches to AI at the Classroom Level

Innovative tools can be used in transactional ways that diminish results. Consider a student who decides to apply AI tools in the most transactional way possible: to complete assignments. Then, place that student in a classroom of a teacher who has embraced the transactional use of AI tools to more efficiently design lessons, create assessments, and grade student work. This leads to a scenario where the teacher uses AI tools to design assignments, the student uses AI tools to complete the assignment, and the teacher uses an AI tool to grade the assignment. The result? What started as a quest for transactional efficiency became a process of two unwitting groups of data entry specialists tweaking algorithms to improve an AI model's automaticity. The end result is work completely devoid of relevance, integrity, or meaning. The transactional obligation of trading tasks for points has been fulfilled, but no learning has occurred.

These examples reveal some truths about a leader's role in helping others navigate change:

- When innovative tools allow people to reach for quick, transactional fixes, they will be eager to do so.
- Absent the opportunity to develop new understandings related to long-held assumptions about the nature of the work, a transactional application of old strategies to innovative tools may be seen as the only possible next step.
- The misalignment of a transactional approach applied to a second-order challenge can create new problems that undermine the capacity for effective teaching and learning.

To avoid such pitfalls, consider these tips from Senge's (2006) work on addressing systems-level challenges:

- Acknowledge that "problems" that emerge when using AI tools may have more to do with our own existing mental models, choices, and strategies than with the tool itself.
- Focus on understanding the root causes of problems and you'll be able to spend less time urgently reacting to symptoms. To get at the root cause, look beyond the surface-level explanation (students are using AI to cheat) and seemingly easy solution (therefore, stronger consequences are needed). Instead, repeatedly ask, "Why?" (*Why do students cheat? Why are they overwhelmed?* etc.).
- Don't confuse more effort with effectiveness. More effort only produces better results if it is intentionally aligned to more effective strategies or addresses the root cause of a problem.
- Don't confuse efficiency with effectiveness. Greater efficiency is a mirage unless it is accompanied by improved results.

Transformational Approach

Consider the following scenario.

A principal convenes the school's policy committee to discuss the issue of students using AI to cheat on assignments. As the committee reviews the school's current academic dishonesty policy, they focus on the section that reads as follows: "Any outside assistance that provides an unfair advantage or any failure to properly cite and acknowledge sources is a violation of the policy and will result in a failing grade for that assignment."

After some discussion, the committee chair says, "Well, I guess we don't need to change anything; we just need to actually enforce the policy as it's written." There are nods of agreement around the conference table.

"We still need to address *why* students are cheating," says the principal. "Are AI tools the problem, or has students' use of AI tools revealed some faulty assumptions we've been making about cheating and academic integrity all along?"

"I have some thoughts on that," a committee member adds. "Some of our students go home to parents with master's degrees or have full-time tutors and access to apps that check their math and correct their grammar. Is that outside assistance providing an unfair advantage? We all ask students to provide written responses to all sorts of questions on their homework, but aside from research papers in English, do we ever ask students to cite sources? Maybe AI isn't the problem. Maybe we need to look at the policy with new eyes."

A few months later, the committee has developed a draft of a new academic integrity policy as well as a document titled "Our Shared Commitment to Academic Integrity." The revised integrity policy includes consequences for dishonesty, but also clarified definitions of important terms, encourages teachers to establish clear boundaries for the use of AI tools, and states that students must transparently acknowledge the use of tools and outside sources when completing assignments. The "Shared Commitment" document articulates ways teachers can support students' efforts to act with integrity, what students can do to take greater ownership of their learning, and what parents can do to help students find balance among school, family, and extracurricular responsibilities.

After the policy and guiding document became official, the chair of the professional learning committee approached the principal.

"I was talking with the chair of the policy committee about holding a joint committee meeting later this year," he says. "We'd like to work together to plan some professional learning on strategies that support academic integrity and reduce cheating. I was sharing some ideas with her about how to affirm help-seeking behavior, reduce cognitive load on assignments and assessments, and teach students to use AI tools for formative assessment and retrieval practice. She was intrigued and I told her I'd ask you if we could bring both groups together. We're really working toward the same things."

The principal smiled and replied, "I think that would be fantastic."

This scenario illustrates a transformational approach aligned to the complexity of the second-order change. Rather than seeing cheating with AI as a transactional issue to be fixed with greater consequences, the principal created conditions where staff were challenged to identify the root causes of the problem and understand the situation in new ways. The principal and the committee modeled the capacity to be flexible, innovative, and open to change. Finally, because the chairs of the two committees realized their work was mutually supportive, they needed to work together to support the new ways of thinking and the implementation of new strategies to support the intended change.

Action Step 2: Ask Big, Transformational Questions

The questions we are asked can determine the answers we give. When navigating second-order change, it is important to be aware of the assumptions that underlie our questions and the questions we are asked about AI (Frontier, 2023).

Status quo questions are based on the premise that we need to take action to maintain the system and strategies as they currently exist. For example:

- Who will ensure students can't access AI tools on the local network?
- Where should we add references to "AI" in the current academic integrity policy?

The underlying assumption in these questions is that the problem and solution are known; what is needed is a decision.

Transactional questions are based on the premise that existing beliefs, skills, and strategies are effective, but different incentives or resources are necessary to improve results. For example:

- What new AI tools for teaching are available, and do we have the funds for licenses?
- Should a new tech person be hired who can just focus on AI?
- What plagiarism-detection tool can we use to catch students who are cheating?

Each of these questions is based on the premise that AI has disrupted the existing order, created a gap in existing capacity, or created an opportunity, and a transaction needs to occur for that gap to be repaired or opportunity to be filled. When answering these questions, sometimes a simple yes or no answer will suffice. But in a period of second-order change, we may need to look beyond the transactional premise of the questions and reframe them to better align with the organization's transformational needs.

When navigating second-order change, it can be difficult for leaders to acknowledge that they don't have all the answers. Absolve yourself of this responsibility. The very nature of second-order change is that answers and solutions that had worked in past may no longer be relevant. In fact, to help others navigate transformational change, one of the most powerful things a leader can do is not answer questions, but *ask* big, transformational questions—those that challenge long-held assumptions, invite new ways of thinking about the nature of the work at hand, and help others break free from the past. Consider, for example, the following transformational questions related to AI:

- What does it mean for students to understand, and what do we accept as evidence of understanding when a student has accomplished a task independently? Supported by others? Supported by technology?
- What parameters should be put in place to ensure that AI tools are used in ways that are aligned to our mission, our shared beliefs, and our shared priorities for teaching and learning?
- How should AI tools be used—or not used—for different purposes, such as to meet foundational goals (learning to read, numeracy), acquire content knowledge (facts, academic vocabulary), or develop conceptual understanding (explaining relationships, justifying one's reasoning)?
- Why do students engage in forms of academic dishonesty despite knowing it is wrong and that they will face consequences if caught? What are the implications of our answers for our teaching?
- If an AI tool could provide individualized, one-on-one instruction to students every day, what characteristics of effective teaching would we most want it to utilize?
- What skills and strategies will students require to be intentional learners in an era of AI?
- What opportunity gaps for historically underserved learners can finally be addressed with AI tools? What gaps might widen? What should we do?

- What components of effective teaching could be effectively replaced by AI tools? What components should *not* be replaced by AI tools? What are the benefits or drawbacks of each, and why?
- If a teacher's likeness, voice, speech patterns, knowledge, and skills can be automated to interact with numerous students at any time through AI, what are the implications for students and teachers?

When faced with transformational challenges, it is not a leader's job to absolve others from reality and preserve the status quo. Nor is it the leader's job to give immediate, easy answers that provide transactional, surface-level solutions to the complex issues at hand. A leader's job is to build the capacity of those within the organization to better meet the needs of those the organization serves. One way to do this is to ask big, transformational questions that challenge existing assumptions and stimulate discussions that challenge and support the new ways of thinking that are necessary to navigate second-order change.

Action Step 3: Place Purpose and Pedagogy Before Technology

John Maeda, an artist and academic who currently serves as vice president of design and AI at Microsoft, frames the difference between a technologist and a humanist this way: while the technologist says "I do because I can," the humanist says "I do because I care" (Maeda, 2006). He continues:

> The default motto of the technologist is that more technology is better .... With just the switch of one letter for two, technology can become humanized. I hope that *care* prevails over *can* for the next few years while we weather the utter complexity of the systems that surround us.

In my book *Teaching with Clarity* (Frontier, 2021), I argue that teachers and students are mired in a debilitating amount of clutter because *can* has tended to prevail over *care*. We have access to more information and resources than ever before. There is an unspoken assumption that if we access more information, do more, and cover more, students will learn more. But this is false. Generative AI's capacity to push out even more information—and students' capacity to use AI to complete their work with just a few keystrokes—could accelerate this problem. If we cared more, we'd prioritize developing what Greg McKeown (2014) calls "the discipline to do less." In an era of unlimited access to information and unlimited capacity to generate information, a teacher's ability to help students prioritize their efforts to intentionally learn needs to be at the center of any conversation about effective teaching.

To teach with intention is to create clear alignment between purpose and pedagogy. To be clear about purpose means designing units, assessments, and assignments with the end in mind and knowing what it means for students to demonstrate evidence of understanding (Frontier, 2021). To be clear about pedagogy means designing lessons with our students in mind so we can align our strategies for teaching to their needs. To place purpose and pedagogy before technology means showing care for our students by helping them prioritize their strategy and effort to learn. If we aren't clear about our purpose for teaching, we have no business putting AI-generated resources in front of students simply because we can.

Action Step 4: Provide Opportunities for Low-Stakes Practice and Play

In his book *Deep Thinking* (2017), world chess champion Garry Kasparov shares insights about the limits and potential of both human and artificial intelligence. In 1997, Kasparov lost a chess match to IBM's chess-playing AI computer, Deep Blue. In the 1980s, well before most people thought it would ever be possible for a computer to beat a human in chess, Kasparov noted that laptop computers had already started to change how elite chess players would practice their craft:

> Many older players found [laptops] too complicated, too alien, especially after having decades of success with their traditional training and preparation methods. How professional chess changed when computers and databases arrived is a useful metaphor for how new technology is adopted across industries. . . . Being young and less set in our ways definitely makes us more open to trying new things. But simply being older isn't the only factor that works against this openness—there is also being successful. When you have had success, when the status quo favors you, it becomes very hard to voluntarily change your ways. (Kasparov, 2017, p. 60)

Kasparov's wisdom can be applied to teachers, too. Although younger teachers may feel more comfortable interacting with AI tools and be more open to trying new things than their more experienced peers, they may not understand the complexities of designing effective curriculum, instruction, and assessment. On the other hand, while experienced teachers know what worked well in the past and can draw on a nuanced language of curriculum design, they may be less willing to try new approaches or new technology tools than younger teachers.

Leaders can create opportunities for both new and experienced teachers to work together to draw on one another's strengths. I've found that once someone has a general sense of how to prompt AI tools, there are only two things they need to do to use them effectively: (1) unlearn their mental models of how to interact with technology when there is no human on the other side of the screen and (2) apply a nuanced vocabulary from a specific academic discipline or domain of expertise to prompt AI tools with specificity. To these ends, one way to demystify AI tools is to give teachers a chance to play with them. Play provides opportunities for people to experiment with ideas, skills, and strategies in a way that is both intentional and enjoyable (Ong, 2020).

One strategy I recommend is to have teachers work in pairs to "play" with AI tools by doing the following:

- **Ask the AI tool a question.** Prompt the AI tool with a question about a topic that is of interest to you. Follow up with specific clarifying questions. Example: "What do you know about _____? Can you tell me more about _____?"

- **Challenge the AI tool.** Push back against a specific point the AI tool makes, regardless of whether the point is accurate. Example: "In your previous response you said '_____.' I am not sure that is accurate. Are you sure you are correct on that point?"

- **Chat with the AI tool.** Engage the tool in a back-and-forth discussion about a topic of interest to them. Example: "I'm trying to decide between _____ and _____. Can you engage me in a discussion to weigh the pros and cons of each?"

- **Ask the AI tool to quiz you on a topic you know well, but pretend to be a novice.** Example: "I've just learned about _____. Can you give me a quiz to see how well I know the basics? Don't give me the answers. Correct my quiz and give me feedback after I'm done."

- **Ask the AI tool to quiz you on a topic you don't know much about at all.** Ask the same question as in the preceding strategy, but this time choose a complex topic that you don't know much about.
- **Test the limits of what the AI tool knows it can or cannot know.** Examples: "What am I going to have for dinner tonight?" "Who will win the World Series in the year 2049?"
- **Test the limits of how the AI tool responds to illogical prompts.** Examples: "What year did Franklin Roosevelt sign the Declaration of Independence?" "My first-graders are struggling with complex functions in calculus—what do you recommend I do?"
- **Be creative with it.** Example: "Write a song about _____ in the style of _____."
- **Be serious with it.** Examples: "Here are four multiple-choice questions from a recent assessment. Can you tell me the correct answer for each item and provide your justification as to why that item is correct?" "Next week I'll be teaching my students in grade _____ about _____. Tell me some common misconceptions students have about this topic, then provide a bulleted list of four strategies that I can use to address those misconceptions."

After playing around with these prompts, pairs can share responses that they think are particularly interesting with others. Then, have each pair discuss and record their thoughts on the following takeaways:

- *A-has*—What surprised you? What did you learn?
- *Uh-ohs*—What concerns do you have about what you observed?
- *Hmmms*—What questions do you now have about when and how AI tools should be used to support effective teaching and learning?

The purpose of this activity is not to determine if AI tools are "good" or "bad" but to allow both naysayers and technology enthusiasts to develop a shared understanding of the strengths and limitations of these tools and how they might be used to support effective teaching and learning.

Questions for Reflection and Discussion

1. What distinguishes a transformational approach to navigating change from a transactional one, and why is a transformational approach necessary in an era of ubiquitous access to AI tools?

2. What does it mean to align leadership behaviors to the magnitude of change?

3. What are some examples of status quo, transactional, and transformational approaches to the second-order change represented by AI?

4. What is a big, transformational question that you could ask about using AI tools in school to challenge long-held assumptions, invite new ways of thinking, or help others break free of routines or strategies that may now no longer be relevant?

5. What does it mean to place purpose and pedagogy before technology? What are the implications for leadership decisions about the use of AI tools in school?

6. How can low-stakes play help teachers with more pedagogical expertise and teachers with more technological expertise work with and learn from one another about the capacity, form, and function of AI tools?

Emphasize Integrity
Align Expectations for Academic Integrity with Intentional Opportunities to Learn

Student access to generative AI tools created a sense of urgency among educators related to concerns about cheating (Meckler & Verma, 2022). However, two years after the release of ChatGPT 3.5, rates of student cheating remained unchanged. This isn't good news; before and after the release of ChatGPT, a staggering 65 percent of students reported that they'd cheated in the previous month (Lee et al., 2024). While rules and consequences must be a part of a school's efforts to deter cheating, these approaches alone fail to address the root causes of the problem. How can we ensure students are intentionally taught, and given the opportunity to intentionally learn, the skills and strategies required to demonstrate academic integrity?

Cheating vs. Academic Integrity

The research on the perceptions and prevalence of cheating in schools can be summed up by the title of a study that was done more than 20 years ago: "It's Wrong, But Everybody Does It" (Jensen et al., 2002). Recent research shows little has changed. Drawing on data from over 70,000 high school students collected across more than a decade of research, the International Center for Academic Integrity (2020) found that 95 percent of students admitted to participating in some form of cheating. Even prior to the release of ChatGPT, students were adept at using technology to cheat. For example, one study from 2019 showed that the typical student knows more ways to cheat using technology than the typical teacher is aware is even possible (Burgason et al., 2019). The same study also found that a large percentage of students who cheat do not view their behaviors as violations of academic integrity.

AI tools have made cheating easier for students. One way educators have attempted to deter cheating with AI is through the use of AI detection tools. While these tools can be part of a broader strategy, they are imperfect (Bjelobaba et al., 2023) and "too easy to game" (Weber-Wulff et al., 2023, p. 30). Further confounding the issue, teachers are overly confident in their ability to accurately identify AI-generated text (Fleckenstein et al., 2024). Given that AI detection tools and educators are both fallible when it comes to detecting AI-generated text, a more comprehensive approach is necessary.

In this chapter, I use the terms *cheating* and *academic integrity* intentionally:

- **Cheating** is the use of a tool or resource to misrepresent one's knowledge and skills to receive undue credit for a task. An accusation of cheating needs to be supported by the accuser with evidence that cheating occurred.
- **Integrity** describes a commitment to ensure one's completion of a task accurately represents the knowledge and skills one actually possesses. A claim about integrity is supported by the learner's ability to 1) transparently document the resources or sources used to engage in one's work and 2) explain or expand on their evidence of learning.

This distinction is important. I reviewed more than 50 different middle and high school academic integrity policies in the last year. In nearly every case, the title of the policy had little to do with its text. The title and opening sentence claimed to be about integrity, but the text only discussed examples of, and consequences for, cheating. Telling students what not to do is not the same thing as teaching students what to do (Culatta, 2021). If we value academic integrity, students will need to be taught the skills and strategies required to demonstrate academic integrity.

Behaviorism vs. Humanism

Behaviorist approaches to policy assume that rewards will affirm, and therefore increase, desirable behaviors and punishment will decrease unwanted behaviors. A school rooted in a humanist approach, by contrast, will begin by trying to understand and proactively address the underlying reasons for students' behaviors. The humanist educator asks, "What legitimate needs are students trying to fulfill, and how can I proactively address them?"

The Behaviorist Approach

The biggest tools in the behaviorist's policy toolbox are the transactional elements of *rules* and *consequences*. Figure 3.1 shows an example of an academic integrity policy that uses a decidedly behaviorist approach.

While this policy effectively defines key terms and shares important clarifying examples, consider the following drawbacks of the policy shown in the figure:

- **It fails to frame the issue in terms of what students should do.** The policy is titled "Academic Integrity," but it focuses entirely on the consequences for cheating. The policy doesn't clarify what it means or how to act with integrity.

FIGURE 3.1 NON-EXAMPLE: A BEHAVIORIST ACADEMIC INTEGRITY POLICY

Academic dishonesty, cheating, or plagiarism will not be tolerated. Students caught engaging in any form of academic dishonesty will be given an *F* and will be subject to disciplinary action.

Definitions of Key Terms

- Cheating is obtaining or attempting to obtain an unfair advantage on assignments or assessments. Cheating involves the possession, communication, or use of technology, information, materials, notes, or other resources that are not authorized by the instructor.

- Plagiarism is the use or reproduction of ideas, words, statements, code, images, etc. created by another person or generated by a technology tool without specific acknowledgment, clear attribution, and proper citation.

Some examples of cheating include:

- Copying another student's work, in part or in whole, without a teacher's permission

- Using any notes or other resources on an assessment without teacher permission

- Sharing or receiving answers, questions, or any portion of an assessment in advance

Some examples of plagiarism include:

- Copying text directly from a source without providing proper quotation marks and a proper citation

- Paraphrasing text without attributing it to the source and/or not providing a proper citation

- Presenting any phrases, sentences, paragraphs, code, images, charts, etc. that aren't your own without attribution and a proper citation

Use of Artificial Intelligence (AI) Tools

As related to issues of cheating and plagiarism, AI-generated text, images, code, audio, visuals, etc. are external sources and do not represent a student's own knowledge, skills, or understanding. Therefore, the use of any AI-generated material in one's own work is subject to policies for cheating and plagiarism and will result in an *F* and being subject to disciplinary action.

(Note the critique of this solely behaviorist approach in the text.)

- **It sends mixed messages about what plagiarism is and is not.** Students are frequently told to use information directly from textbooks or other assigned materials as the source of answers for their daily schoolwork. However, it is typically only on major papers or projects that students are asked to mention, let alone formally cite, the sources they use. This means the majority of the time, teachers affirm student work that is uncited yet substantially similar to, or directly taken from, the source text, which is otherwise the very definition of plagiarism. This seeming contradiction can be confusing for students.
- **It fails to acknowledge the complexity of unfair advantages.** What constitutes an "unfair advantage"? Tutoring? Using an AI tool? The support of a parent with expertise in the subject? What about using an app that provides homework support for a monthly fee, or a word-processing add-on that serves as an embedded writing editor and coach?
- **It fails to adequately integrate AI.** Rather than being thoughtfully integrated into the policy, AI is tacked on at the end like an afterthought.
- **It fails to understand the form and function of AI.** The clause about AI at the end of the policy implies that students can only use AI tools the same way they use other online resources: by searching them for content that they then cut and paste into their own assignments. But what if students use an AI tool to create a slide presentation based on their original written work or to solicit feedback and make suggested edits?

If identifying punishments for cheating were enough, issues of academic integrity would have been resolved long before the advent of AI. While rules and consequences must be a part of a school's efforts to ensure academic integrity, a solely behaviorist approach fails to address root causes and is insufficient to help students and teachers navigate the challenges of ubiquitous AI in schools.

The Humanist Approach

In contrast to behaviorism, humanist theories such as expectancy-value theory (Atkinson, 1964; Eccles, 1984; Wigfield & Eccles, 2000) and self-determination theory (Ryan & Deci, 2000) can be used to consider students' needs as learners and create conditions that support academic integrity.

Expectancy-value theory (Atkinson, 1964; Eccles, 1984; Wigfield & Eccles, 2000) is based on the premise that students make rational decisions when determining whether to invest effort in a task, weighing

- Expectancy, or the extent to which a student believes they can successfully accomplish a task; and
- Value, or the extent to which the outcome of the task is important to the student.

In a perfect scenario, the student's expectations and value are positive and well-aligned. They are confident that they can complete an assigned task, which is just challenging enough to keep the student's interest, but not so challenging that they feel overwhelmed. And, because the student sees value in successfully completing the task, they invest effort accordingly.

By contrast, consider a scenario when expectations and value are not aligned. A student expects to do poorly on an important task that has been assigned a high value toward their final grade. The student rationalizes three options: not do the assignment and get a low grade, muddle through and get a low grade, or cheat and get a high grade. The student decides the third option is the only way to align expectations for success with the valued outcome. Expectancy-value theory doesn't mean we condone this decision. It helps us better understand, and more proactively address, the factors that underlie a student's decision to cheat.

A humanist approach to academic integrity based on *self-determination theory* (Ryan & Deci, 2000) would consider how to support learners' needs for autonomy, competence, and relatedness:

- **Autonomy** is the need to feel a sense of control of one's behaviors and choices. Students' sense of autonomy is supported when we give them choices and allow them to decide how to use their time or approach a task. Autonomy is undermined when students feel threatened or coerced or when they believe expectations must be followed even though they are irrelevant or arbitrary.
- **Competence** is the need to believe one has the skills and abilities necessary to accomplish important tasks. Students' sense of competence is supported when tasks are at an appropriate level of challenge and students have enough time and access to resources to complete them. Competence is undermined when tasks are too challenging or expectations for success are inconsistent, vague, or arbitrary.
- **Relatedness** is the need to feel a sense of connection and belonging with others. Students' sense of relatedness is supported when they feel accepted and cared for. Relatedness is undermined when individuals believe they are in competition with others or feel rejected or unworthy of being accepted for who they are.

Acknowledging these human needs gives us a more comprehensive view of the challenges students face when navigating issues of cheating. Consider, for example, the potential implications of these needs on students' internal narratives:

- If a student believes a task is too difficult, they may rationalize cheating as a way of exercising autonomy to complete the task.
- If a student sees other students cheating, they may rationalize doing it themselves through the relational lens of "everybody does it."
- If a student's friend asks for help in a manner that violates expectations for integrity, the student may comply to avoid jeopardizing their relationship.
- If a student gets stuck while trying to complete a task, they may decide to cheat, rather than ask for help, because they fear they will be judged as incompetent or unworthy of acceptance.

None of these narratives justify academic dishonesty. But that doesn't mean they are irrelevant. A humanist approach acknowledges the reality of these internal conflicts and seeks to leverage relatedness, competence, and autonomy as central—rather than tangential—to empower students to act with integrity.

Given the discussion on expectancy-value theory and self-determination theory in the previous section, it shouldn't be surprising that researchers (Pope & Schrader, 2023) have found that students are less likely to cheat when they

- Have opportunities to provide input into their learning experiences and can use low-stakes, formative assessments to align their strategy, effort, and results.
- Feel a sense of belonging to a community that values integrity and effort.
- Believe the teacher cares about them and their learning.
- Care about their teacher's opinion of them.
- Are invested in furthering their own learning and see their assignments as helping them do so.

Action Steps: Emphasize Integrity

To take a humanist approach to policies and practices that support academic integrity, follow these action steps:

1. Take a learning-based approach to support academic integrity.
2. Articulate expectations for staff, students, and families to support academic integrity.
3. Clarify the parameters for when and how AI tools should be used.
4. Ensure integrity, transparency, and explainability of evidence of learning.

Action Step 1: Teach Content, Concepts, and Skills Related to Academic Integrity

If we want students to demonstrate the knowledge and skills required to meet high standards for academic integrity, we'll need to teach them intentionally. This can be done by

- Establishing clear, school-wide expectations for how to demonstrate academic integrity.
- Using class time to teach important integrity-related vocabulary (e.g., *integrity, plagiarism, intellectual property*), technical skills (e.g., paraphrasing, quoting), and abstract concepts (e.g., fair use, common knowledge, attribution). Then provide students with formative opportunities to practice, develop, and apply their knowledge and skills.
- Utilizing consistent expectations for integrity across courses. This could include procedures for communicating what resources can or can't be used on various assignments, expectations for transparency and explainability (which will be explained in Action Step 4), and both when and how to cite sources.
- Promoting classroom practices that emphasize the learning process, such as the use of formative assessments and developmental feedback, scaffolding larger assignments into smaller steps, and providing advanced notice for tests and projects.

Action Step 2: Articulate Expectations for All Stakeholders to Support Academic Integrity

Too often, students are expected to independently interpret and abide by academic integrity policies. Articulating expectations for students as well as administrators, teachers, and parents or guardians can ensure all stakeholders know the important roles they play and the actions they can take to support academic integrity. For example:

Administrator Responsibilities

- Work collaboratively to establish a clear and comprehensive policy that aligns expectations for academic integrity with the school's mission and purpose.
- Provide information and resources to all stakeholders to communicate the importance and value of academic integrity.

- Provide professional learning to build teachers' capacity to support students' efforts to act with integrity.
- Ensure the policy is followed, as articulated, in a manner that is consistent, timely, objective, and fair.

Teacher Responsibilities

- Communicate the importance of academic integrity as an essential element of the learning process.
- Plan units and lessons that provide students with the opportunity to learn the content and skills necessary to accomplish assignments and assessments.
- Provide students with advanced notice of due dates and break major assignments into smaller steps.
- Create clear parameters related to what resources students can or cannot use for specific assignments or assessments.
- Use instructional time to teach, provide models, and discuss how to act with integrity and avoid dishonesty, cheating, and plagiarism.
- Integrate questions about transparency (e.g., *Can you share the steps you followed to engage in this work?*) and explainability (e.g., *Can you explain the relationships among the most important ideas in your work?*) as a normal part of instruction.
- Affirm students' efforts to seek help, ask questions, and respond to feedback.
- Follow up with administrators on concerns related to, or possible violations of, academic integrity.

Student Responsibilities

- Participate in class activities, complete assignments, and ask questions to support your learning.
- Seek clarification if you are unsure about instructions and/or deadlines.
- Manage your time to ensure you complete assignments and are prepared for assessments.
- Follow expectations related to what resources can and cannot be used on specific assignments, and transparently document your use of resources or sources as required.
- Understand the school's definitions of academic integrity, plagiarism, and cheating, and ask your teachers for clarification if you are unsure about a decision or choice you need to make.
- Demonstrate honesty and integrity in your decisions and actions.

Parent/Guardian Responsibilities

- Be familiar with and supportive of the school's academic integrity policy.
- Support students' positive choices, growth, and sense of responsibility for their own learning.
- Encourage students to see productive struggle and perseverance as essential parts of the learning process.
- Encourage students to seek help from teachers as needed and to advocate for their own learning needs.
- Help students balance their pursuit of academic, extracurricular, social, and personal interests with their physical and emotional well-being.

Action Step 3: Clarify the Parameters of When and How AI Tools Can Be Used

Clear parameters related to when and how technology tools can or cannot be used ensure the integrity of assessment evidence and empower students to act with integrity. Consider some of the questions students may have—but not ask—about when it is appropriate to use AI tools such as those shown in Figure 3.2.

By anticipating and clarifying answers to questions like these, teachers and students both benefit. Teachers can ensure they are making accurate inferences about their students' skills and understandings when looking at students' work. Students are empowered to exercise their autonomy to use AI tools in ways that are aligned with expectations for integrity. Of course, it is always acceptable to tell students they must complete a task without any assistive technology at all.

Action Step 4: Emphasize Integrity, Transparency, and Explainability

In the past, academic integrity meant being honest about doing one's own work and citing sources. The age of generative AI will further blur the lines between what students appear to have accomplished and what technology has accomplished for them. This requires employing some additional elements to ensure that completed tasks accurately reflect student understanding. To this end, I believe students should become accustomed to sharing evidence of—and having conversations about—evidence of integrity, transparency and explainability:

FIGURE 3.2 EXAMPLES OF QUESTIONS STUDENTS MAY HAVE ABOUT THE APPROPRIATE USE OF AI TOOLS

Questions About Process	Can I use AI to . . . • Develop ideas or an outline? • Ask for feedback on work I've completed? • Study for an upcoming assessment? • Break a long-term task or project into smaller steps?
Questions About Acquiring Content Knowledge	Can I use AI to . . . • Summarize an assigned reading? • Make a complex reading task more accessible? • Generate content? • Ask for help about content I don't understand?
Questions About Products	Can I use AI to . . . • Answer homework questions? • Write an essay? • Create a slide presentation from my original work? • Create charts or graphs? • Create visuals, audio, or video?

- *Integrity* means being honest about doing one's own work and properly acknowledging information, ideas, skills, products, or quotations that can be attributed to others.
- *Transparency* means being clear about steps taken and resources used (e.g., books, tutors, AI tools) to complete any assigned task.
- *Explainability* means being able to expand on, justify, or clarify one's work or answers.

Prompts to facilitate conversations around these important elements can be used formally as a part of assignments or assessments or informally through discussions with students to validate the integrity of their evidence of understanding:

Prompts for Students to Demonstrate Integrity

- *How does your work accurately represent your independent thinking and understanding of the topic?*
- *How have you credited the ideas, words, or work of others on this assignment?*

Prompts for Students to Demonstrate Transparency

- *What process or strategies did you use to complete or prepare for this assignment?*

- *List any resources—including individuals, books, or AI tools—that you used and provide printouts of any prompts used with (and responses received from) AI tools.*

Prompts for Students to Demonstrate Explainability

- *Now that you've completed this assignment, what do you think are the three most important things to know about this topic and why?*
- *Summarize the most important ideas in your work with a few concise sentences.*
- *Select an original quote from your writing that you are most proud of. Write the quote, and then explain your thinking in more detail. How does it fit into the larger structure of your essay?*

From a behaviorist perspective, the only reason to ask questions or have conversations about integrity, transparency, or explainability with students would be to use them as evidence to catch them cheating. That would be a travesty. These are powerful questions that show interest in students and build their capacity to be reflective learners. In a system that values intentional learning, we should engage our students with these types of questions all the time.

Questions for Reflection and Discussion

1. What are the characteristics of a humanist, rather than behaviorist, approach to school policy?
2. How might a solely behaviorist approach to academic integrity undermine effective teaching and learning?
3. How might a humanist response to academic integrity support effective teaching and learning?
4. How does a learning-based approach help minimize cheating and build students' capacity to act with integrity?
5. How might a school community benefit from clearly articulating expectations for the role of administrators, teachers, students, and families to support academic integrity?
6. How does creating clear parameters for students' use of AI tools support academic integrity and ensure teachers can make accurate inferences from students' evidence of learning?
7. What are integrity, transparency, and explainability? How can shared attention to these elements support effective and intentional teaching and learning?

Fidelity Before Efficiency
Use AI Tools to Support Intentional Teaching and Learning

AI tools hold tremendous potential to support efficiencies and automate routine teaching tasks. This could allow educators to spend more time engaged in high-leverage practices to support students' learning. However, decisions to use AI tools come with opportunity costs. For example, AI tools could automate elements of the teaching process in ways that diminish teachers' understanding of students' learning needs. Or, AI tools could be used in ways that allow teachers to create instructional resources more efficiently, but those resources don't have fidelity to students' learning needs. How can educators use AI tools in ways that support efficiencies *and* ensure effective, intentional teaching and learning?

The Challenge of Teacher Burnout

A recent study found teachers feel overworked and overwhelmed at rates higher than other professions due to such factors as increased workloads, extreme politicization, and broader societal challenges (Gershensen & Holt, 2022). Another study found that 58 percent of teachers reported experiencing "frequent job-related stress," 56 percent reported feeling "burnout," and 23 percent reported they were "likely to leave their job by the end of the school year" (Doan et al., 2023).

Given these challenges, it's no surprise that after the initial release of ChatGPT 3.5, many educators were interested in how AI tools could be used to create efficiencies and provide some relief.

However, before reaching for those AI tools, it is important to also consider the perceptions of the 77 percent of teachers in the study cited above who reported they were *not* likely to leave their job. These respondents cited their "ability to positively affect students," their "positive relationships with students," and "other teachers" as the top reasons they intended to stay. Seen through a lens of humanism (see Chapter 3), one way to interpret this is that despite the challenges teachers face, those who are satisfied in their roles feel a strong sense of *competence* and *relatedness*. What if teachers' use of AI tools increases their efficiency while undermining their sources of satisfaction? Any discussion about how AI tools can be used to *automate* or create *efficiencies* in the teaching process also warrants a discussion of the potential impact of AI tools to diminish teachers' sense of autonomy, competence, and relatedness.

The following terms will be used throughout this chapter and in the chapters that follow to consider how to balance the opportunities and opportunity costs of using AI tools when teaching.

- **Fidelity**—The alignment of a student's learning needs to a teacher's use of effective strategies.
- **Opportunity to learn**—The alignment of priorities for teaching to opportunities for students to effectively apply, adjust, and develop, their knowledge and understanding of important content, concepts, and skills.
- **Efficiency**—The relationship between the amount of effort put forth and the amount of work accomplished.
- **Automaticity**—The routine application of an action or process, without the need for conscious thoughts or monitoring, to accomplish a task.
- **Effectiveness**—The alignment and use of specific teaching strategies that consistently support the attainment of specific goals and measures associated with increased student learning.
- **Expertise**—The intentional alignment and nuanced application of teaching strategies that are used in the right way, at the right time, across a variety of contexts, to consistently support increased student learning.

Fidelity

In some circles, the term *fidelity* is used to mean "lockstep adherence to a preexisting curriculum." I disagree with that approach to teaching; a lock-step curriculum undermines teachers' autonomy and minimizes their ability to be responsive to students' learning needs. I also disagree with that characterization of the term *fidelity*.

When educators teach with fidelity, students can trust that they'll be provided with intentional opportunities to align their efforts to develop a deeper understanding of what is most important for them to learn. Similarly, when students engage in the learning process with fidelity, it means teachers can trust them to invest meaningful effort in their learning and present work that accurately represents their current level of skill and understanding. Fidelity reflects the essence of the teacher-student partnership; there is a shared understanding of where we are right now, where we are going, and the path to get there. AI tools have the potential to be used in ways that undermine fidelity.

For example, suppose students are given a task related to a learning goal that requires them to compare ideas articulated in two documents written at an 11th grade level of text complexity. Abigail is home working on the assignment that night and she finds the text in the two documents to be confusing. Ever the mindful student who prides herself on acting with integrity, Abigail looks at the assignment: *Compare and contrast documents A and B by answering the following questions.* In her mind, it's the content knowledge, not the reading skill, that is the purpose of the assignment. She uploads the two passages to an AI tool and asks for a summary. After doing this, she prints the summaries and uses them to answer the questions in the assignment thoughtfully. The next night, while grading student work, the teacher looks at Abigail's answers and writes a few comments commending her for the quality of her work. The teacher noticed that several students struggled with the task. For these students, he provides some specific developmental feedback, posts a link to a mini-lesson, and shares a resource for navigating complex text. These students are asked to watch the mini-lesson, apply one of the strategies, and revise an answer of their choice.

Because Abigail's evidence of learning lacked fidelity to her actual skills and abilities, the teacher's response lacked fidelity to her learning needs.

Teacher Expertise

Experts use the right strategy in the right way at the right time to get the results they desire (Frontier & Mielke, 2016; Marzano et al., 2011). Expertise is more than effectiveness or competence. Expert performers consistently elicit exceptional results because they are able to

- perceive meaningful interconnected patterns missed by others in their field,
- process relevant information to engage in important tasks more efficiently than their peers,
- recognize important challenges in their domain at a deeper level than others,

- spend more time than others applying strategies to address those challenges, and
- continuously self-monitor to effectively align effort and strategy to intended results (Chi et al., 1988).

How Teachers Develop Expertise

Expertise is not synonymous with experience (Marzano et al., 2011). Competent teachers may have plenty of experience, but after an initial steep learning curve early on, their skills may become stagnant as they learn to rely on the same few strategies to attain acceptable results. Experts, on the other hand, engage in what Ericsson calls "deliberate practice" (Ericsson, 2006; Ericsson & Pool, 2016): they objectively monitor and reflect on the impact of their strategies. Then, they turn that reflection into action by making precise modifications to improve their ability to use that strategy more fluently and effectively. Over time, they develop a nuanced ability to apply a repertoire of strategies that can be used to consistently afford their students opportunities to attain exceptional results.

If skills and strategies that are associated with the struggle, reflection, and deliberate practice of expert teaching are automated by AI tools, teachers' capacity to develop expertise may suffer. Consider the following list of tasks that represents just a fraction of the work many teachers have to do each year:

- Develop standards-aligned unit plans, lesson plans, assignments, and assessments that are developmentally appropriate for learners.
- Create connections with students to understand their social-emotional needs and establish trust.
- Teach engaging, standards-aligned lessons that capture students' attention and focus students' strategy and effort to learn.
- Provide meaningful feedback to guide students' acquisition of content knowledge, deepen their conceptual understanding, or help them develop important skills.
- Reflect on students' evidence of learning as feedback about their own teaching to affirm or inform their own next steps to better support students' learning.
- Provide students with additional opportunities to learn through reteaching, conferring, assigning small-group work, or holding review sessions.
- Evaluate student assignments and assessments, grade student work, enter grades, and determine final grades.

- Communicate with parents or students by writing e-mails, announcements, or newsletters.

With these tasks in mind, consider the following questions:

- What tasks can be automated by AI tools to create more time for teachers to invest their effort in developing their expertise and providing high-quality opportunities to support student learning?
- What tasks could be automated by AI tools but could ultimately undermine teachers' expertise or minimize their understanding of their students' learning needs?
- How might teachers use AI tools to more efficiently complete routine or repetitive tasks so they can spend more time using higher-leverage strategies that support student learning?
- How might teachers use AI tools to more efficiently complete important—but time-intensive tasks—in ways that don't diminish their understanding of students' learning needs?

These are big, transformational questions without easy answers, but they are precisely the types of questions that need to be asked in an era of second-order change. Our answers to these questions will have a profound impact on both teachers' expertise and students' learning.

Action Steps: Fidelity Before Efficiency

To help educators find the right balance among fidelity, efficiency, automaticity, and expertise, follow these action steps:

1. Avoid the "twin sins" of efficiency or automaticity without fidelity.
2. Engage in dialogue about fidelity, efficiency, automaticity, and effectiveness.
3. Take an expert's approach to using AI tools intentionally.
4. Ensure fidelity, transparency, and explainability of resources for teaching.

Action Step 1: Avoid the "Twin Sins" of Efficiency or Automaticity Without Fidelity

To explore the challenge of balancing fidelity and efficiency in an era of ubiquitous access to AI tools, let's begin by considering an already widely used technology: the learning management system (LMS). This is an efficient way for teachers to assign, receive, grade, and give feedback on student work. However, this technology can also undermine the impact of feedback: One recent study found that when students using an LMS could see their grade on a writing assignment, only 55 percent bothered reviewing any additional feedback (Laflen & Smith, 2017). As the title of another related study puts it, students often take a "check the grade, log out" approach to using an LMS (Winstone et al., 2020). An LMS is an efficient tool for delivering feedback, but it may undermine the potential of feedback to improve students' learning.

With that opportunity cost in mind, consider the following scenarios:

- A teacher uses an AI tool to design an assignment and uploads it to an AI-enabled LMS, which automatically assigns it to students. After students complete their work (assume their work was actually done with integrity for this example), they submit it to the LMS, which uses AI to automatically score it and generate written feedback. Both the score and the feedback are then automatically shared with the student.

- A teacher uses an AI tool to generate a rubric for an upcoming project that includes research, writing, and a student presentation. After typing a few quick prompts into an AI tool, the teacher now has a rubric for each of these three components. At a glance, the rubrics look great. The teacher posts them to the class website for his students to consult the next day when they will be assigned the project. A few days later, a student asks the teacher a question about the rubric. After reviewing the rubrics more closely, the teacher realizes each element on the rubric has more to do with surface-level elements of the task and following directions than with important, standards-aligned success criteria. In fact, the success criteria are disconnected from the purpose for which the task was assigned.

The first scenario above exemplifies the use of AI to automate teaching: the routine application of a process without the need of conscious monitoring to accomplish a task. From the outside looking in, the approach appears effective; work has been assigned and completed, and grades and feedback have been given. But the teacher is unaware of how the students responded or where individual students may have gotten stuck. Because the teacher doesn't have a faithful understanding of how students performed, she's diminished her capacity to respond with fidelity to their needs. Additionally, the automation in this scenario will have a negative impact on the teacher's capacity to develop expertise. She's automated the conscious monitoring—and opportunities for reflection, modification, and deliberate practice that experts use to continuously improve.

The second scenario exemplifies the use of AI to create efficiencies; the teacher was able to put forth less effort to accomplish more work in less time. However, the benefits of these efficiencies were short-lived, as the success criteria generated from the AI tool did not have fidelity to important goals for learning. Even if students acted with integrity as they engaged in the project, their scores would not be a faithful representation of their progress toward important standards. With a tip of the hat to Grant Wiggins and Jay McTighe's "twin sins" of instructional design (2005), these scenarios are examples of what I call the "twin sins" of integration of AI tools for teaching:

- **Automaticity without fidelity** occurs when tasks are automated in a manner that undermines teachers' capacity to understand or be responsive to students' learning needs.
- **Efficiency without fidelity** occurs when efficiencies are gained in terms of effort or time required to produce instructional resources for students, but those resources aren't aligned to priorities for teaching and/or to students' learning needs.

The result of the twin sins? Diminished capacity for teachers to support students' learning and to develop expertise. It is worth reiterating that these sins refer to the misapplication of AI tools, not to any issues with the AI tools themselves. The twin sins clarify what not to do. As teachers reach for AI tools to automate tasks and create efficiencies, the goal is to do so in ways that ensure

- Routine tasks are automated in a manner that frees teachers and students to invest effort in more intentional teaching and learning, and
- Efficiencies gained help teachers and students spend more time engaged in higher-leverage strategies or opportunities that improve their capacity to effectively teach and learn.

Action Step 2: Engage in Dialogue About Fidelity, Efficiency, Automaticity, and Effectiveness

In the film *Jurassic Park*, Professor Ian Malcolm shares an observation that is worthy of reflection and conversation in the context of AI tools: "Your scientists were so preoccupied with whether or not they could, they didn't stop to think if they should." Now that data scientists have made AI tools accessible

FIGURE 4.1 SAMPLE QUESTIONS FOR EXPLORATORY DIALOGUE ABOUT EDUCATORS' USE OF AI TOOLS

Questions About Capacity	• What can teachers do that AI tools can't do? • What can AI tools do effectively that most teachers can't do? (e.g., translate languages, transcribe student presentations) • What can AI tools do more efficiently than a teacher can do? (e.g., find patterns in students' misconceptions on 120 paragraph-long written responses, generate exemplar and non-exemplar responses as aligned to different levels of success criteria)
Questions About Fidelity	• If teachers use AI tools, how can they be used to ensure the fidelity of instructional strategies or resources to priorities for intentional teaching? • If students use AI tools, how can they be used to ensure the fidelity of students' efforts to learn to goals for intentional learning?
Questions About Opportunities for Efficiency and Auto-maticity	• What routine, logistical tasks typically completed by teachers should or should not be automated by AI tools? • What tasks related to intentional teaching should or should not be done with AI tools?

Questions About Opportunity and Opportunity Costs	• If an AI tool is used to perform or augment a logistical task, develop instructional resources, or apply teaching strategies, how might that positively or negatively impact:
	   – Teachers' and students' sense of autonomy, competence, or relatedness?
	   – Teachers' and students' fidelity to shared priorities for intentional teaching and learning?
	   – Students' expectations that productive struggle leads to success?
	   – Students' application of aligned learning strategies?
	   – Teachers' application of instructional strategies and development of further expertise?

to everyone, educators have a responsibility to discern and determine gaps between what AI tools can do and how, when, and whether they should be used. Consider using the questions in Figure 4.1 to guide an exploratory dialogue among educators on this topic. Start by focusing on capacity, then pivot, in order, to fidelity, efficiency, automaticity, and opportunity costs.

After discussing the questions in Figure 4.1, educators can consider the extent to which AI tools should be used to develop instructional resources, design units and assessments, and assess student work by reflecting on the questions in Figure 4.2. Though the answers to some of the questions in Figure 4.2 may be a straightforward yes or no, others may be determined to be acceptable only under specific conditions or with specific caveats. For example, perhaps a committee decides it's appropriate to use AI tools to generate learning goals, but only if they are based on grade-level standards.

FIGURE 4.2 CONVERSATION STARTERS ABOUT APPROPRIATE USES OF AI TOOLS

Questions About Developing Resources	Should teachers use AI to . . . • Generate differentiated materials to make content more accessible to students? • Generate summaries or explanations of academic content? • Revise required readings to make them easier for students to read? • Translate instructional materials into different languages? • Generate instructional videos, slide decks, or presentations? • Generate newsletters for parents about what is happening in their classroom?
Questions About Instructional Design	Should teachers use AI to . . . • Generate ideas for units or lesson plans? • Generate learning goals? • Generate rubrics and success criteria? • Generate exemplars and non-exemplars? • Create unit or lesson plans? • Generate ideas for classroom activities or projects? • Generate assignments? • Plan for modifications and accommodations per an IEP? • Generate assessment items? • Generate entire assessments?
Questions About Assessment	Should teachers use AI to . . . • Score student work on multiple-choice assessments? • Assess student work on open-ended assignments or assessments? • Provide whole-group feedback to students about patterns of weakness or strength in work samples? • Provide individual students with feedback? • Assign students' grades? • Write letters of recommendation?

If the answer to any of these questions is yes,
• How can you ensure that AI tools are used or prompted in ways that maintain fidelity to priorities for intentional teaching and learning?
• Is it appropriate to automate these processes or assign them to AI agents?

The intent of these questions is not to be transactional or punitive. They are a starting point for engaging in dialogue around real-world decisions while navigating the ambiguity of second-order change. Boundaries and constraints can be limiting, but they also empower teachers to be confident that they are using AI tools in ways that will be supported by administration. This frees up teachers' capacity to explore and determine how AI tools can create efficiencies or automate tasks in ways that help them manage their workload, build their expertise, and help their students learn.

Action Step 3: Take an Expert's Approach to Using AI Tools Intentionally

Experts are deeply intentional about fidelity: they use tools strategically to ensure intended results. Whether they're artists, mechanics, doctors, or teachers, experts clarify their purpose before reaching for a tool and putting it to use. Clarity of purpose ensures they intentionally

- Select the most appropriate tool;
- Determine the strategies to use and how to apply them to the tool most effectively; and
- Discern whether the tool, and how it is being used, is producing the desired results.

To help teachers determine if, and how, to use AI tools, consider the following questions to help them clarify their purpose:

- What are the most important goals for students' learning?
- What is the most important evidence that will show that students have learned?
- What are your students' most important needs as learners?
- What instructional resources and teaching strategies will you use to most effectively focus your students' learning? And how—and for how long—should that resource or strategy be used?
- How will you monitor the impact of the instructional resource and teaching strategies on students and modify how you're using them as necessary, in real time, to ensure the intended results?
- How will you ensure integrity, transparency, and explainability of students' evidence of learning to ensure accurate inferences about their level of skill and understanding?

Notice that these questions are AI agnostic. They represent the type of questions that experts teachers reflect on as habits of mind to intentionally align purpose, effort, and strategies to tools or resources in order to attain desired results.

Action Step 4: Ensure Fidelity, Transparency, and Explainability of Resources for Teaching

In the previous chapter, I discussed the importance of transparency and explainability to support the integrity of *students'* evidence of learning.

Similarly, transparency and explainability can be used to support the fidelity of *resources for teaching* that have been developed using AI tools. Consider the following definitions as related to the development of resources for teaching:

- **Transparency** means being clear and open about the processes used to plan learning experiences, generate instructional resources, develop assessments, assess student work, and determine grades.

- **Explainability** means you can explain the meaning of, and rationale for including, any elements from instructional resources, assessments, projects, and rubrics that were designed whole or in part using AI tools.

Attention to questions such as those that follow can inform or demonstrate the intentionality of one's teaching and assuage stakeholders' concerns about how AI tools or resources are being used to support intentional learning.

Questions Teachers Can Use to Plan for, and Reflect on, Fidelity

- *What important content, concepts, and skills should students know and understand by the end of this unit?*

- *How have assessments and rubrics been aligned to important standards and learning goals?*

- *How will students have formative opportunities to learn important content, concepts, and skills across this unit?*

- *If AI tools were used to generate resources, how were they reviewed, edited, or revised to ensure accuracy and alignment with curricular priorities and students' specific learning needs?*

- *If AI tools were used to assess student work, how did you verify the accuracy and reliability of the feedback or scoring?*

Questions Teachers Can Use to Reflect on Transparency

- *What specific resources—including individuals, books, and technology—were used to plan curriculum, instruction, and assessments in this unit?*

- *If AI tools were used, what prompts were used to develop instructional resources, lessons, assignments, or assessments?*

Questions Teachers Can Use to Reflect on Explainability

- *How did you intentionally design this unit/assignment/assessment to scaffold students from more basic, to more complex, evidence of understanding?*
- *How does this assessment provide you with important evidence of students' knowledge and understanding as related to prioritized standards?*
- *If AI tools were used, can you explain the meaning of any—and all—output that was shared with students?*
- *If AI tools were used to provide feedback to students, can you explain the meaning of the feedback that was given to each student?*

In an era of AI, these questions can help ensure teacher autonomy and AI can coexist. For example, after discussing Action Steps 2 and 3 in this chapter, a schoolwide committee on teachers' use of AI could decide to put just a few hard limits in place for how AI should *not* be used. Then, they could agree that beyond those limits, teachers can use AI tools at their discretion as long as they've transparently documented their use, can explain the output, and can justify how that output has fidelity to priorities for teaching and learning.

Questions for Reflection and Discussion

1. Define *fidelity, efficiency,* and *automaticity.*
2. What is teacher expertise and how is it developed?
3. How might the use of AI tools to create efficiencies or automate some aspects of the teaching process but undermine teacher's capacity to develop expertise?
4. What are the "twin sins" of integrating the use of AI tools in school? How might they impact teachers' and students' success?
5. What factors should teachers consider when attempting to balance automaticity and efficiency with fidelity?
6. How can attention to fidelity, transparency, and explainability support teachers' intentional, effective use of AI tools?

Teaching, Learning, and AI

Guiding Principles and Action Steps to Use AI Tools to Support Intentional Teaching and Learning

5

Stand in Their Shoes
Empathize with Students' Perceptions of AI Tools and Learning

Students' beliefs about learning determine how they invest effort to learn. When productive beliefs are intentionally aligned to effective strategies, students flourish. Unfortunately, students hold many misconceptions about how learning occurs (Brown et al., 2014). These misconceptions can lead to the use of strategies that undermine students' well-intended efforts to learn. Students' use of AI tools could deepen these misconceptions or result in uses of AI tools that undermine their learning. By taking an empathetic approach to acknowledging these challenges, we can take more intentional action to support students' learning needs.

Empathetic vs. Non-Empathetic Design

Empathy is the ability to imagine oneself in another's shoes to better understand and value their perceptions and feelings. Teachers demonstrate empathy by being aware of, acknowledging, and acting in ways that are responsive to their students' perceptions—and misconceptions—of schooling and learning. In contrast, a non-empathetic approach rests on the assumption that learners see lessons, content, assignments, and technology tools just as we do.

An empathetic approach to designing learning experiences for students begins with the premise that students' perceptions matter. John Hattie's (2012) conclusion drawn from his synthesis of meta-analyses of educational research that learning occurs most effectively "when teachers see learning through the eyes of the student and when students see themselves as their own teachers" (p. 238) speaks to the importance of a student-centered design approach. The essence of the first part of this elegant quote is *empathy*. But its elegance belies the obstacles that teachers need to overcome to see their content and classrooms from their students' perspective.

Set Your Shoes Aside: Acknowledge the Curse of Knowledge

Before we can stand in the shoes of our learners, we need to set our own shoes aside. This means we need to let go of our assumptions about the content, concepts, and knowledge that, in our own minds, are simple and self-evident. This act of empathy is so difficult to do that there is a name for it: "the curse of knowledge" (Heath & Heath, 2006).

The *curse of knowledge* is the cognitive bias of *not* being able to remember what it was like to *not* understand facts, concepts, and skills that we've already internalized. Paradoxically, more knowledge can be an impediment to effective teaching. Consider the following:

- Teachers bring extensive content knowledge and highly specialized skills to their disciplines that they have built through years of coursework.
- Teachers with many years of experience revisit, re-teach, and, by extension, review the content, concepts, and skills in their curricula on an annual basis.
- When teaching a class over a period of years, teachers are able to find efficiencies in the presentations, lectures, activities, assignments, and assessments they use to teach content, concepts, and skills that are entirely new to students.

These experiences bolster our fluency in our disciplines and efficiency in our teaching. But, they can make it more difficult to understand the needs of our students because they can diminish our capacity for empathy.

The *curse of knowledge* creates a deep empathy gap with real-world implications for curriculum design (Brown & McDaniel, 2014; Newton, 1990). In addition to routinely overestimating students' depth of background knowledge and grasp of academic language, educators tend to underestimate the time it will take students to develop an understanding of content and the amount of confusion they'll experience when attempting seemingly routine tasks.

By setting our shoes aside and acknowledging that our disciplinary expertise can be an impediment to empathy, we can better position ourselves to stand in the shoes of our students.

Moving from Judgment to Inquiry

When we see students make decisions that undermine their learning, we can be quick to judge them for not applying the strategy, effort, and knowledge that—in our own mind—was obvious. Given their failure to follow our internal script, we can resort to a non-empathetic voice of judgment as the only plausible explanation for their actions: *they don't care, they don't take their time, they are choosing to fail* (see the first column in Figure 5.1).

An empathetic approach, on the other hand, begins by asking why students might have made those decisions in the first place. Consider the following:

- Students have to keep track of assignments and assessments from six or seven teachers across six or seven disciplines in 30 to 40 different classes per week.

FIGURE 5.1 EMPATHETIC VS. NON-EMPATHETIC INTERNAL VOICE

Non-Empathetic: Voice of Judgment	Empathetic: Voice of Inquiry
• "These students are lazy; they just use AI to do their work." • "These students are irresponsible; they just want to rush through everything." • "These students don't read; they just skim for the answer." • "Some of my students care so little, they don't even try." • "I gave my students that assignment a month ago; they ignored it until the last minute, panicked, and then asked AI to do it for them." • "These students know plagiarism is wrong, but they decide to do it anyways."	• "What misconceptions might my students have about the distinction between 'completing tasks' and 'engaging in meaningful learning'?" • "How might students have been conditioned to rush through their work, and how can I support their use of strategies to slow down and be more mindful?" • "How can I help students read more closely and purposefully?" • "What experiences in the past may have caused some students to see a disconnect between effort and results?" • "What conditions prevent students from asking for help and managing their time, and how can I support their efforts to do oth?" • "What opportunities to learn, formative assessment, and developmental feedback have students had about plagiarism and how to avoid it?"

- In any given week, students navigate hundreds of pages of text or links to digital content whose purpose is to introduce them to hundreds of new ideas, vocabulary words, concepts, and skills across the arts, sciences, and humanities.
- Students have instant access to billions of web pages and millions of images and videos via personal electronic devices and the internet.
- Students hold numerous misconceptions about how learning occurs, mistake surface-level knowledge for understanding, and tend to rely on the same few strategies for learning.
- Students have access to AI tools that can efficiently generate correct answers to assigned questions and summarize, synthesize, analyze, and complete assigned tasks.
- Adolescents' frontal lobes are a work in progress. Executive functioning skills governed by the prefrontal cortex don't reach full maturation until about the age of 25 (University of Rochester Medical Center, 2024).

Given these facts, we shouldn't be surprised that students will turn to AI to lighten their load.

By shifting from an internal voice of judgment to one of inquiry, we can better acknowledge and understand how the expectations students face each day, their past experiences, their perceptions, and their misconceptions inform their decisions. This allows us to more intentionally take action to address—rather than miss or dismiss—their underlying needs. Examples of questions that invite reflection and empathetic inquiry are shown in Figure 5.1.

Action Steps: Stand in Their Shoes

To take an empathetic approach to your students in an era of AI, follow these action steps:

1. Acknowledge that students hold misconceptions about learning.
2. Acknowledge that AI could deepen students' misconceptions about learning.
3. Acknowledge that students' misconceptions will influence how they use AI tools.
4. Take action to address students' misconceptions about learning.
5. Affirm students' strengths, challenges, and interests.
6. Take action to minimize cognitive load.

Action Step 1: Acknowledge That Students Hold Misconceptions About Learning

Students hold numerous misconceptions about how learning occurs and about their capacity to learn. Consider the following.

Common Misconceptions About How Learning Occurs

The Fallacy of Mere Repetition

One deeply held misconception about the learning process is that repeated exposure to complex content will result in deeper understanding (Brown et al., 2014). In reality, surface-level strategies such as cramming for a test or re-reading text over and over without doing anything with that information produce little or no long-term advantages for learning. By acknowledging this misconception, we can help students apply more effortful, and effective, strategies that require them to organize, categorize, or synthesize content and concepts in more meaningful ways.

The Illusion of Understanding

People tend to be overconfident in their ability to explain concepts or apply skills to which they've had only surface-level exposure. This misconception is known as "the illusion of understanding" (Rozenblit & Keil, 2002). By acknowledging that "most people feel they understand the world with far greater detail, coherence, and depth than they really do" (p. 522), we can help students slow down, self-identify and articulate gaps in their understanding, and engage in the messiness of transferring what they've learned to open-ended, authentic tasks.

The Illusion of Skill Acquisition

While there are advantages to watching a teacher or an expert on YouTube fluently engage in a complex task, doing so can also foster the "illusion of skill acquisition" (Kardas & O'Brien, 2018): The more often we watch someone perform a complex task with ease, the more likely we are to overestimate our ability to accomplish that task. What learners benefit from most is actually engaging in the task. Unfortunately, once a learner realizes how challenging a task actually is, most learners are quick to give up. By acknowledging the illusion of skill acquisition with our students, we can affirm their frustration and then clarify that their struggle doesn't mean they can't do the task, but rather that they need to break the task into smaller components to practice isolated strategies and incremental steps.

A Feeling of Learning Rather Than Actual Learning

Deslauriers and colleagues (2019) compared the learning of 149 students in two different teaching contexts: a passive, lecture-based approach versus an active, inquiry-based approach. Just prior to taking a summative test, the two groups of students were asked how they thought they'd do on it. Students in the lecture-based setting were more confident but scored lower, and the reverse was true for students in the other group. According to the researchers, these findings indicate that

> when students experience the increased cognitive effort associated with active learning, they initially take that effort to signify poorer learning. That disconnect may have a detrimental effect on students' motivation, engagement, and ability to self-regulate their own learning. (p. 1)

To acknowledge this paradox, students need to hear repeatedly from teachers that their questions and productive struggle are evidence that they are engaging in the process of learning.

"What You See Is All There Is" (WYSIATI)

The phrase "what you see is all there is" was coined by Nobel Prize–winning economist Daniel Kahneman to explain why learners are often wildly overconfident about inaccurate or invalid conclusions. As Kahneman explains,

> You cannot help dealing with the limited information you have as if it were all there is to know. . . .. Paradoxically, it is easier to construct a coherent story when you know little, when there are fewer pieces to fit into the puzzle. Our comforting conviction that the world makes sense rests on a secure foundation: our almost unlimited ability to ignore our ignorance. (2011, p. 88)

Too often, students see accomplishing work quickly or knowing the right answer immediately as evidence of deep understanding. By acknowledging this misconception, we can help students slow down, use strategies that help them identify inconsistencies or errors, and design learning experiences that give them opportunities to access additional information and revise their thinking.

Common Misconceptions About One's Capacity to Learn

Fixed vs. Growth Mindset

Students who believe skills and understanding are a function of natural abilities and that there is little that they can do to improve them have what Carol Dweck (2006) calls a "fixed mindset." Students with a fixed mindset who get stuck when trying to learn tend to have a *coping response*: they avoid challenges, give up easily, or dismiss the work as being unfair.

By contrast, students who believe they can improve their skills and understanding with persistent effort applied to effective strategies have what Dweck calls a "growth mindset." When students with a growth mindset get stuck, they engage with a *thriving response*: they apply a different strategy, modify their effort, and are willing to try again until they've internalized the new understanding or skill.

By acknowledging that a student's mindset can determine the effectiveness of their response, we can more intentionally apply instructional approaches that affirm the intentional alignment of effective strategies with focused effort—rather than innate ability—as the long-term determinant of success.

Error Avoidance

Too often, students see errors or mistakes as classroom kryptonite. They fear errors prove they aren't smart, or believe their clarifying questions will upset their classmates because they slow down the pace of instruction. As psychology professor Janet Metcalfe explains, this is unfortunate because "errors enhance later memory for and generation of the correct responses, facilitate active learning, stimulate the learner to direct attention appropriately, and inform the teacher of where to focus teaching" (Metcalfe, 2017, p. 484). To address students' misconceptions about errors, teachers should communicate messages and apply strategies that affirm a culture of learning where mistakes are honored as an important part of the learning process that can serve as a catalyst for deeper learning.

Learned Helplessness

People who believe there is no relationship among effort, strategy, and results can fall into a state of *learned helplessness* (Seligman, 1972). For example, suppose a learner tries to complete a task a few times and is not successful, so they ask the teacher for help. The teacher says the task is really simple and quickly demonstrates how to complete it. The learner tries again, and when they still don't succeed, they give up in frustration. A week later, the learner is given a similar task. This time, they don't even bother trying. Rather than learning how to complete the task, the student has internalized the belief that he is not capable of doing so. Acknowledging the reality of learned helplessness can help us be more empathetic when supporting learners who have given up.

Learning as Magic

Magicians strive to conceal the relationship among strategy, effort, and results, leaving the audience to conclude that magical abilities are the only plausible explanation for what they've seen. They avoid transparency to make explainability impossible. When we rush to cover content or model skills for students without intentionally revealing and explaining the strategies we are using, we can affirm the misconception that learning is magic. By acknowledging this misconception, we can more intentionally direct students' attention to the strategies that make learners successful. For example, students of all ages benefit from hearing teachers engage in think-alouds, where the teacher vocalizes the thought processes and internal dialogue being used to successfully engage in a task.

Now that you've read about these common misconceptions, revisit the examples of non-empathetic versus empathetic internal voice in Figure 5.1. What are some ways you've mistakenly judged or drawn erroneous conclusions about students because they hold these misconceptions? How could you reframe the non-empathetic voice of judgment into an empathetic voice of inquiry?

Action Step 2: Acknowledge That AI Will Deepen Students' Misconceptions About Learning

Generative AI tools are adept at delivering complex output without revealing any strategies or effort. Students' use of AI tools could affirm misconceptions and create further confusion about the strategy, effort, and productive struggle necessary to learn. For example:

- Because AI tools can provide instantaneous answers to very specific questions or direct students to multimodal demonstrations of specific skills, students may be more susceptible to the *illusion of understanding* and the *illusion of skill acquisition*.
- Because AI tools can provide instantaneous answers to specific prompts in a manner that implies the answer was obvious, they can leave students with even larger gaps between *feelings of learning versus actual learning*.
- Because AI tools can provide perfectly concise answers to specific questions that could previously only have been developed by reviewing multiple resources, students can be further subjected to the over-simplification bias of *"what you see is all there is."*
- Because AI tools can instantly provide answers without revealing strategy, students may conclude that skills related to reading, writing, logic, math, and the arts are innate and magical, resulting in a *fixed mindset* and *learned helplessness*.

Before moving on, take a few minutes to reflect on the following questions:

- What are some implications of these statements for how AI tools should—or should not—be used by students?
- What are some implications for your efforts to ensure intentional teaching and your students' efforts to engage in intentional learning?
- How can you help address misconceptions students may have about learning?

Action Step 3: Acknowledge That Students' Misconceptions Will Influence How They Use AI Tools

Students' misconceptions about learning can have a detrimental effect on how they apply strategy and effort. Figure 5.2 shows how these misconceptions could result in superficial uses of AI tools in ways that undermine their learning. How might an empathetic approach help you more intentionally address some of these challenges?

FIGURE 5.2 STUDENT MISCONCEPTIONS ABOUT LEARNING ALIGNED TO RATIONAL (BUT ERRONEOUS) CONCLUSIONS ABOUT USES OF AI

Misconceptions About Schooling	Erroneous Conclusion
If the purpose of school is to complete tasks and accumulate points . . .	. . . then I'll use AI tools to complete my assignments and accumulate as many points as possible.

Misconceptions About Understanding	Erroneous Conclusions
If knowing facts is the same thing as understanding . . .	. . . then I can ask an AI tool who, what, where, and when questions, and then I'll understand.
If reading something means I understand what I've read . . .	. . . then I'll ask an AI tool to summarize what I'm supposed to read and I'll save time.
If the purpose of math is to receive a problem and get the right answer . . .	. . . then I'll ask an AI tool to solve the problem for me and show its work, and I'll copy what I see.
If more information is better . . .	. . . then I'll use an AI tool to generate information quickly and easily.

Misconceptions About Ability	Erroneous Conclusions
If intelligence in a subject area is innate . . .	. . . then if I struggle or I am confused, it is evidence of inability. Since I'm not good at this subject, I'll just get answers from an AI tool.
If asking questions is a sign of inability . . .	. . . then I shouldn't ask questions in class. I could ask questions of AI tools, but I shouldn't tell my teacher because my teacher will think I'm a cheater.
If mistakes or errors are a sign of inability . . .	. . . then it doesn't make sense to reveal my inability to my teacher. Rather than muddle through and make errors, I can use an AI tool to avoid them.

Misconceptions About Effort	Erroneous Conclusions
If learning is supposed to be easy . . .	. . . then I'll use an AI tool to expend minimal effort. If I still don't understand, it means I'm not capable.
If more effort always results in deeper understanding . . .	. . . then if I studied hard but still did poorly on the test, I must not be capable. I'll use AI on some upcoming assignments to get those points back.

Misconceptions About Technology	Erroneous Conclusions
If technology is better than the human hand or the human mind . . .	. . . then I'll save time by simply having an AI tool accomplish tasks for me.
If generating output using technology means I have acquired a skill or understand content . . .	. . . then AI is an efficient way to acquire and demonstrate understanding.

Misconceptions About Assessment	Erroneous Conclusions
If the primary purpose of assessment is to hold me accountable and reward or punish me with grades . . .	. . . then I'll use AI to efficiently complete these transactional tasks.
If the purpose of feedback is to judge me or to justify grades . . .	. . . then it is my teacher's job, not mine, to reflect on my work.

Action Step 4: Take Action to Address Students' Misconceptions About Learning

Addressing student misconceptions requires the use of strategies that support deep, conceptual changes in thinking (Lucariello, 2015). Some examples of strategies that can be used to take action to address misconceptions about learning include the following:

- Take the time to teach your students about the misconceptions discussed in this chapter, and give students opportunities to reflect on how they've resulted in their misapplication of strategies or the misuse of resources. Discuss the complexity of the learning process and the relationship between strategy and effort with students. Then, use instructional strategies that engage students in the active process of meaning making (see McTighe & Silver, 2020, for detailed examples of these types of strategies).

- Model your internal thinking for students through think-alouds to reveal the internal dialogue you use to make decisions about how to apply strategy and effort. Give assignments that require students to annotate their thinking when doing their work rather than just recording their answers.

- Use intentional teaching strategies that align expectations for learning with the opportunity to learn (see Hattie, 2023).

- Develop a classroom culture where errors are welcomed, questions are valued, it's okay to make mistakes, and productive struggle is seen as an important part of the learning process.

- Point out to students that understanding cannot be "given" by an AI tool any more than it can be "taken" from a teacher. Then use formative strategies that scaffold students' learning experiences to support their growth.

- Give your students permission to call out your "curse of knowledge." Let them know it is okay to say, "We need to slow down" or "I know you know the definition of that word you keep using, but I really don't understand it; can you explain it differently?"

- Affirm the relationship between effort and success with statements such as "This is important and challenging work. With persistence and the right strategies, I am excited to help you make progress."

- Share challenges you've faced as a learner and how you've overcome them. For example: "When I was a student, this confused me, too. I didn't ask my teacher for help because I was afraid she'd think I wasn't capable. Looking back, I wish I'd just asked her to walk me through the steps a few more times."

Action Step 5: Affirm Students' Strengths, Challenges, and Interests

Understanding and affirming students' strengths and challenges allows us to design tasks that meet their needs for autonomy and competence by providing appropriate levels of challenge and support. When we let students know that we are aware of—and not judgmental of—their current skill and ability levels, they are less likely to take shortcuts or resort to cheating. By the same token, knowing our students' interests allows us to develop more supportive relationships and provide relevant examples when teaching. To understand and affirm each learner's strengths, challenges, and interests, consider the following strategies.

Use a Writing Exercise to Gather Baseline Evidence

A simple writing prompt at the beginning of a course can help teachers learn more about students' interests while also establishing baseline evidence of their writing skills. Ask for a fully developed paragraph about something that requires little or no academic knowledge (e.g., favorite hobbies, their ideal school day, what they'd do with 500 dollars). Then, provide feedback for (but don't grade) the baseline evidence with a comment such as "I enjoyed reading your paragraph on (topic) and look forward to working with you this year!" so students know that you are aware of—and accept—their starting point.

Use Interest Inventories

In his seminal book *The Art and Science of Teaching* (2007), Robert Marzano explains the importance of establishing and maintaining effective relationships with students. Inventories that include questions about students' interests and learning needs are a good place to begin. These can include questions such as "How do you like to spend your free time?" or "Who is someone you admire and why?" and "What is something that is important for me to know about you as a learner?" Then, use their responses to engage students in informal conversations or tap into students' interests and expertise throughout the school year.

Gather Feedback to Inform Your Teaching

Asking students for feedback about our teaching demonstrates to them that we are interested in their perspectives, which in turn improves our capacity to teach effectively. Consider asking questions such as these on exit slips or at the end of formative assessments:

- What is something we did that supported your learning?
- What is something you wish I'd done differently to better support your learning?
- What is something I can do to more effectively help you learn?

Action Step 6: Take Action to Minimize Cognitive Load

Cognitive load theory (Sweller, 1988, 2022) can be used to design tasks that minimize the likelihood that students will become overwhelmed, resort to AI shortcuts, or just give up. This can be done by considering three elements when designing tasks. *Intrinsic load* is the amount of mental effort required by students to accomplish a task. This will be dependent on each learner's background knowledge and current skills. *Germane load* refers to the most important aspects of the task. *Extraneous load* refers to elements of the task that are distracting or irrelevant.

To minimize extraneous cognitive load:

- Avoid tasks that require students to integrate new content, new concepts, and new skills simultaneously.
- Ensure that projects and assessments don't emphasize trivial details or bells and whistles over substantive evidence of learning.
- Communicate clear success criteria aligned to relevant standards.
- Make clear that quantity (of pages, slides, problem sets, etc.) does not equal quality.
- Avoid tasks that split students' attention across too many resources.

To maximize germane cognitive load:

- Break larger, more complex tasks into smaller, simpler ones across interim due dates.
- Ensure rubrics draw students' attention to the most important evidence of understanding and success criteria.
- Be specific. For example, if you expect students to use particular terminology in open-response items, provide them with a word bank to use.
- Unless you are focused on a research standard, give students all the resources they need to complete a complex task.

The curse of knowledge can cause us to overestimate the amount of information, resources, and steps a student can handle before they become overwhelmed. To help students manage intrinsic cognitive load:

- Clearly communicate learning priorities and what it means to demonstrate evidence of deep understanding for a given task or course.
- Scaffold tasks to help students move from surface knowledge (identify, recall, describe) to deep understanding (explain, synthesize, justify).
- Allow students to use formative resources such as graphic organizers, outlines, and notes to plan and complete complex work.
- Use class time for student goal setting, self-assessment, and reflection.
- Use consistent formatting for assessments, projects, rubrics, and unit overviews across an entire course.

By standing in the shoes of our learners when designing assignments, assessments, and projects, we can better help them align their strategy and effort to intentionally develop and demonstrate their understanding.

Questions for Reflection and Discussion

1. What is empathetic design and how does it differ from non-empathetic design?
2. What is the curse of knowledge and how can it undermine teachers' efforts to empathize with their students?
3. What does it mean to move from judgment to inquiry? How can doing so help teachers empathize with their learners?
4. Why is it important to acknowledge student misconceptions about learning, particularly in an era of ubiquitous AI tools?
5. How might AI tools further distort students' misconceptions about learning?
6. How can acknowledging that students' misconceptions about learning will influence how they use AI inform teachers' efforts to address root causes and respond more empathetically?
7. How can taking action to minimize cognitive load help students avoid using AI tools in ways that undermine their learning?
8. How can standing in the shoes of your learners help teachers more intentionally understand and meet their needs?

6

Know Your Purpose
Prioritize Students' Strategies and Efforts to Learn

By ensuring that students are clear that the purpose of our classes is to support their learning rather than obtain their compliance, we can more intentionally align our priorities for teaching to our students' investment of strategy and effort to learn.

The Role of Strategy, Effort, and Tools in a Culture of Compliance

In a culture of compliance, students believe the purpose of school is to follow directions, complete assignments, earn points, and get good grades regardless of whether any long-term learning occurs. Given this premise, students see the purpose of assignments, quizzes, assessments, projects, and rubrics as tools the teacher uses to hold them accountable through the allocation of points and grades.

Compliance-driven classrooms are often arranged along a superficial conveyor belt of content where "coverage" is synonymous with teaching and "memorizing" is synonymous with learning. By emphasizing surface-level knowledge that can be assessed as either right or wrong, it ensures points can be allocated fairly and objectively. Compliant classrooms can also be hands-on and active, but the projects and activities often lack rigor because they emphasize surface-level success criteria such as *a two-minute video, eight PowerPoint slides, or five paragraphs*; that can be used to objectively award points for easily observable evidence.

Compliance is an efficient way for students to "do school," but it does little to help students learn. Consider, for example, author Denise Clark Pope's take-away from shadowing and interviewing high school students over the course of a semester for her book *Doing School* (2001):

> [Students] studied the material, read the textbooks, and completed the assignments, for the most part, because they had to, not because they wanted to or because the subjects genuinely interested them. Students often memorized facts and figures without stopping to ask what they meant, or why they were asked to learn the facts in the first place . . . [One student] said most of the facts she had memorized [were then] "emptied out of her brain." She was required to move on to the next assignment to keep up with the pace of class. (pp. 155–156)

Unfortunately, many students still perceive compliance as the purpose of schooling. In a recent study of over 21,000 high school students by Yale University (Moeller et al., 2020), 80 percent of students reported "boredom" among their most common feelings about school. These students have learned to navigate school in a state of "passive compliance" (Schlecty, 2002); they put forth just enough effort to avoid consequences and attain points and grades. Examples of how strategy and effort are applied to classroom resources and tools, including AI tools, in a culture of compliance are shown in Figure 6.1.

The Role of Strategy, Effort, and Tools in a Culture of Learning

In a culture of learning, the teacher emphasizes students' development of strategies and application of effort to accomplish increasingly challenging goals (Anderman & Gray, 2017).

Rather than viewing assignments, assessments, feedback, and rubrics as tools the teacher uses to monitor compliance, students and teachers work together to use these tools to affirm and inform their strategies and efforts to effectively teach and learn. Examples of how strategy and effort are applied by teachers and students to classroom tools and resources in a culture of learning are shown in Figure 6.1.

FIGURE 6.1 PERCEPTIONS OF PURPOSE IN A CULTURE OF COMPLIANCE VS. A CULTURE OF LEARNING

	Culture of Compliance	Culture of Learning
Course	Cover content, assign projects, and earn grades/credit	Spark curiosity and help students integrate, revise, and deepen their understanding of prioritized content, concepts, and skills
Motivation and Goals	Accumulate points and earn high grades (extrinsic)	Deepen understanding and develop new skills (intrinsic)
Focus of Teacher's Strategy and Effort	Present content or facilitate activities	Intentional alignment of priorities for learning with students' opportunity to learn
Focus of Student's Strategy and Effort	Follow course requirements, meet deadlines, memorize content, or follow rote steps	Develop and deepen understanding of content, concepts, or skills
Assessment	Focus on grades and points (summative and transactional)	Guide teachers' and students' ongoing use of strategies to learn (formative and reciprocal)
Teacher Questions	Hold students accountable	Provoke and guide inquiry and help students plan, monitor, and evaluate of their own learning
Student Questions	Clarify rules, instructions, due dates, and grading procedures	Satisfy curiosity and/or better understand content, concepts, or skills
Assistance	Students avoid asking for help because it is seen as evidence of low ability or seek help in the form of "What is the answer?"	Students ask for help to clarify misconceptions or to modify and apply more effective learning strategies
Mistakes or Errors	Students avoid mistakes or errors because points are deducted when they occur	Students see mistakes or errors as part of the learning process and use them to focus next efforts to learn
Feedback	Delivered by the teacher as a summative judgment or to justify a grade	Used by the student to affirm or inform their strategy and effort to learn
Rubrics	Emphasize following directions and quantitative elements that are easily observed, but may be detached from standards; used to justify a grade	Emphasize standards, transferable skills, and important evidence of understanding; used by teachers and students to align intentional teaching to intentional learning
Classmates	Students see classmates as competitors or sources of correct answers	Students see classmates as collaborative partners and as resources to support their learning
Teacher's Use of AI Tools	Create efficiencies or automate content delivery, assignment management, or grading	Create efficiencies to ensure effective, intentional teaching well aligned to students' learning needs.
Student's Use of AI Tools	Find answers or complete course requirements	Support the use of strategies that result in intentional learning
Academic Integrity	Prevent students from cheating and hold them to account	Ownership of one's evidence of learning (transparent and explainable) to ensure the fidelity of teaching strategies to efforts to intentionally learn

Consider the following scenario and subsequent discussion of a classroom that exemplifies a culture of learning.

A Culture of Learning: Ms. Learner's U.S. History Class

Ms. Learner is clear with the students in her history class that her purpose is to help them understand history by learning to think like historians. In addition to teaching facts, she makes sure her instructional strategies and assessments develop students' skills to *contextualize and explain historical events, summarize documents and texts, support claims with evidence*, and *analyze documents for perspective, bias, and factual basis*. In fact, written work and many of the projects in class are formatively and summatively assessed using rubrics based on these exact elements. Her assessments include both multiple-choice items related to important content and open-ended tasks that require students to contextualize events, support claims with evidence, and analyze documents. Ms. Learner also has students self-assess their work with these standards in mind and gives them frequent opportunities to reflect on the relationship between their efforts and results. She ends each assessment in her class with these four questions:

- How did I challenge and support your efforts to be successful in this unit?
- What is something you wish I'd done differently to better support your learning?
- What strategies did you use to learn new content or apply skills more effectively?
- What is something you could have done differently to better support your own learning?

When Ms. Learner uses AI tools to design lessons, assignments, or assessments, she always consults a course framework that includes priority standards, important learning goals, essential questions, and disciplinary strategies. She uses precise language from the standards and the course framework to prompt the AI tool in very specific ways and ensures that any AI-generated materials are aligned to both.

Ms. Learner invests class time in teaching students how to use success criteria. For example, to introduce her students to the four-point rubric they'll use throughout the year for the criterion *supports claims with evidence*, she starts by having students go through the rubric and underline words that represent important distinctions among the different achievement levels, then has them discuss the distinctions as a class. Next, she gives students eight AI-generated paragraphs. (After several iterations of drafts from the AI tool, she was able to prompt it to create two exemplar paragraphs for each of the four levels of the rubric.) Then, in groups, students have to determine how they think each paragraph should be scored and why. This discussion clarifies for students what it means to effectively support claims with evidence. Next, each group revises each paragraph so that it meets the criteria for a level 4 on the rubric. Finally, each student completes this prompt as an exit slip: "To effectively support claims with evidence, it is important to remember that _____." The next day, Ms. Learner returns the slips to students and posts a summary of their statements at the front of the room.

"I want to teach you to accurately self-assess the quality of your own writing," she says. "To do that, you need to practice assessing a lot of good, mediocre, and lousy examples of other's writing. Once you get better at assessing the AI-generated paragraphs, you'll be able to help one another improve your own."

Now that you've seen an example of a culture of learning in action, return to Figure 6.1. Which elements in the second column were evident in Ms. Learner's class? How do you think Ms. Learner might apply any elements that are missing from the scenario in ways that intentionally support student learning?

Action Steps: Know Your Purpose

To help students focus on learning, follow these action steps:

1. Acknowledge that superficial uses of AI tools can harm learning.
2. Avoid the "twin sins" of curriculum design.
3. Emphasize that the purpose of school is learning, not compliance.
4. Teach students to self-monitor and self-assess.
5. Emphasize integrity, transparency, and explainability.

Action Step 1: Acknowledge That Superficial Uses of AI Tools Can Harm Learning

If students believe the purpose of school is to complete tasks in exchange for points and grades, it makes sense that they'd apply strategies to AI tools to efficiently fulfill that purpose (Frontier, 2025). You want me to read a 10-page article? *Prompt: Summarize this article into a paragraph.* Do math problems 1–21? *Prompt: Complete the math problems in the photo attached. Write a five-page essay on* To Kill a Mockingbird? *Prompt: Write a five-paragraph essay from the perspective of a high school students who admires Atticus Finch because of his integrity, honesty, and wisdom.*

The efficiency of these superficial uses of AI tools come at a steep cost for students' learning. Consider the following conclusions drawn from research:

- **Unguided, superficial prompts harm learning.** Students completing assignments using a standard version of ChatGPT typed or pasted the assigned question directly into the AI tool more than 60 percent of the time. In the moment, these students got the correct answers, but after access to the tool was removed, they performed more poorly than students who hadn't used AI on the initial tasks (Bastani et al., 2024).

- **Cognitive ease comes at a cost.** Students reported that using AI tools to synthesize text made their work easier than navigating information across multiple resources, but their final products were assessed as less thorough and of lower quality than those of students who didn't use AI tools for the same task (Stadler et al., 2024).

- **Over-reliance on AI negatively affects students' ability to apply strategies for learning.** By relying on AI tools to find answers or complete tasks, students avoid the productive struggle required to develop a deeper understanding of content and diminish their capacity to navigate complex tasks independently (Zhai et al., 2024).

To create conditions where students can use AI tools in ways that support their learning, we need to ensure students have access to resources and opportunities that allow them to prioritize and align their strategy and effort to learn.

Action Step 2: Avoid the "Twin Sins" of Curriculum Design

According to Grant Wiggins and Jay McTighe (2005), the two design errors that most often impede students' efforts to align strategy and effort to learn are *coverage without understanding* and *activities without understanding*. These are so pervasive they call them the *twin sins* of curriculum design. *Coverage without understanding* occurs when surface-level awareness of content is accepted as evidence of deep understanding. *Activities without understanding* occur when lessons or projects are hands-on, but the tasks don't require students to develop or demonstrate an understanding of important knowledge, concepts, or skills.

As you read the scenarios that follow, think about how you've experienced these design flaws as a student, how you've committed them as a teacher, how they invite passive compliance, and how AI tools could make them even more pervasive.

Coverage Without Understanding

In Mr. Covera's biology class, the syllabus provides details about unit titles, class rules, test dates, and how grades and points are allocated. Across each two-week unit, he lectures and gives his students assigned readings and some comprehension questions for homework. Each day, Mr. Covera asks if students have any questions from last night's homework. There rarely are any. If a question is asked, it is usually about whether something will be "on the test." After he's answered questions, he moves on to the day's lecture. At the end of each unit, students are given a 45-question multiple-choice test about unit content and one open-ended prompt that he has prepped them to answer correctly throughout the unit. When the next unit begins, the process repeats with a new topic and entirely new content. There is no attempt to bring coherence to the course by emphasizing transferable skills or concepts. When a colleague asks Mr. Covera if his students are using AI tools to help with their homework for his course, he proudly replies, "If they take time to read what I give them and do the online practice quizzes, the answers are all right there, so they don't need AI."

Mr. Covera's biology classroom exemplifies the design flaws of *coverage without understanding* in the following ways:

- There is a strong emphasis on covering lists of topics, but no effort has been made to discern what is trivial from what is central to the discipline.
- Because there is no expectation that students do anything with the information presented other than report it back to the teacher, students can do well in the course simply using surface-level strategies to memorize content until it has been tested.
- Telling is accepted as teaching, and students don't have the opportunity to develop and apply strategies that will help them make meaning of what they learn.
- Students' questions are primarily about whether items will be "on the test" because they have no need to ask deeper questions that require conceptual clarification to succeed in the course.

- The course seems to be more about getting the right answer than learning. Whether students "get the answers" from the book, their teacher, or an AI tool, they can succeed in the course without deepening their understanding of content and concepts.

Coverage without understanding is an incredibly efficient way to "do school," but it is a remarkably ineffective way to develop and deepen students' understanding.

Activities Without Understanding

Mrs. Activo has noticed her middle school history students haven't been very engaged. She decides to create some hands-on projects to wrap up a unit on the political structure and history of ancient Greece that they've been working on for the previous month. To generate the projects, she types the following prompt into an AI tool:

> What would be some interesting and engaging projects for my middle school students to do as they learn about ancient Greece?

After its cursor blinks a few times, the AI tool produces the following reply:

Ancient Greece offers a treasure trove of exciting and engaging project ideas that can enrich middle school students' learning experience. Here are some project ideas that can help bring ancient Greek history, culture, and mythology to life:

1. **Greek Pottery Making:** Using clay, students can create their own pottery that mimics the style of ancient Greek vases. They can add figures and scenes inspired by daily life in ancient Greece or famous myths, practicing techniques such as making black-figure or red-figure pottery.
2. **Greek Meal:** Students can select a traditional Greek recipe and prepare it for the class. This can be a great way to help students appreciate different cultures and try something new.
3. **Graphic Novel:** Students can use an app to create their own graphic novel about a Greek myth. This helps with understanding narrative elements and encourages artistic design skills.

These projects can help students engage more deeply with the subject matter of ancient Greece, making the learning process interactive and multifaceted.

Mrs. Activo appreciates that these projects are hands-on and appeal to her students' interests. She realizes she'll need some way to grade them, so she prompts the AI tool to generate a rubric for each project. A few moments later, she has a rubric that includes categories for appearance, design, and creativity. The next day, she shows her students the options and tells them they can choose one of these projects to work on in the next week. Students give her an enthusiastic response.

The next week is chaotic. Students don't know how to manipulate the clay and have no idea how to paint anything other than blobs and stick figures. One student brings in some Greek food—she and her father made a Greek dessert. When Mrs. Activo asks the student about the history of the dessert, she has no idea; "We just followed the recipe," she says. Most students chose the graphic novel project. They looked amazing but lacked substance. Students could generate the entire graphic novel on an AI tool in a matter of minutes by simply selecting some options, dragging and dropping some images, and responding to a series of prompts. As Mrs. Activo reflects on the week, she realizes students asked hundreds of questions about acquiring and using materials, finding resources, time constraints, and deadlines, but not a single clarifying question about the political structure or history of ancient Greece.

Mrs. Activo has the right intentions, but this scenario has all the trappings of *activities without understanding*. It's great that the AI-generated activities are hands-on and engaging, but they are ineffective for many reasons:

- They are not designed with any standards or specific learning goals in mind.
- They are time-, skills-, and resource-intensive, and students are bound to spend more time on making sure their product looks (or tastes) good than on applying and deepening their understanding of content and concepts central to the unit.
- Even if the products appear to be of high quality, they offer no evidence that students have learned the knowledge, concepts, or skills that were the intent of the unit.
- The success criteria emphasize aesthetic elements that are detached from important course outcomes. Because of this disconnect, students may see

the tasks as busy work and may be more likely to seek shortcuts that violate expectations for integrity.

School should be hands-on and engaging. Projects and performance assessments support student autonomy and can be used to tap into their interests. However, autonomy without attention to students' needs to develop competence in important goals for learning undermines students' motivation. When designing activities, strive for a balance between active engagement and intentional opportunities to learn.

Preventive Strategies

The "twin sins" invite passive compliance because they fail to align intentions for teaching with opportunities to learn. To minimize the likelihood that the use of AI tools will result in coverage without understanding or activities without understanding, avoid the following (in the next chapter, detailed guidelines will be shared about what *to do* to prompt AI tools in ways that support intentional teaching and learning):

- Avoid the use of assignments, worksheets, projects, assessments, or rubrics that have been generated from AI tools based on prompts that failed to clarify important details about priority standards and important learning goals.
- Avoid the use of activities that have been generated from AI tools that require students to apply knowledge and skills that haven't been taught in the course.
- Avoid the use of rubrics or success criteria that have been generated from AI tools using prompts that failed to clarify the most important, standards-aligned attributes of quality.
- Avoid the use of AI tools to generate resources that already exist. For example, why have an AI tool compose a letter home from a soldier in World War II when there are thousands of such letters available online?
- Be careful not to use AI tools in a manner that amplifies misconceptions, biases, or distorts facts (e.g., by presenting fictional dialogue from a real-life historical figure).

Action Step 3: Emphasize That the Purpose of School Is Learning, Not Compliance

To transcend the twin sins and align intentions for teaching with students' opportunities to learn, Wiggins and McTighe (2005) remind us that we need to *begin with the end in mind.* By identifying, articulating, and applying the following components as resources that teachers and students use to guide their efforts, we can better support students' efforts to focus on deep learning of important content rather than gaining compliance through superficial uses of AI tools.

Organize Courses and Units Around Priority Standards

If students see school as being organized around homework, quizzes, projects, and tests, they will never move out of "AI is a tool for compliance" mode. In a culture of learning, teachers use standards to intentionally guide their instruction and students use them to intentionally guide their learning. By focusing on a limited number of transferable standards, teachers and students can focus their strategy and effort on goals for learning rather than just completing tasks. Examples of transferable standards include the following:

- Develops claims using evidence to support reasoning.
- Constructs clear explanations.
- Analyzes and interprets data.
- Makes sense of problems and perseveres to solve them.

These are examples of transferable standards because they occur across courses, units, and lessons. Students can use them to both develop and demonstrate evidence of understanding by meeting specific learning goals. (See Figure 6.2 for an example of alignment of an activity and set of learning goals to a priority standard.)

Use a Shared Language of Rigor

A consistent language of rigor can focus efforts to scaffold students from surface knowledge (knowledge of facts and rote application of skills as aligned to goals and tasks that include verbs such as *identify, define,* and *follow steps*) to deeper understanding (fluent, flexible application of content, concepts, and skills to open-ended tasks as aligned to goals and tasks that include verbs such as *synthesize, argue,* and *justify*). A framework such as Structure of the Observed Learning Outcome or *SOLO* (Biggs & Colis, 1978) or Bloom's Taxonomy (Anderson et al., 2001) can be used to reliably unpack standards, articulate learning goals, and then intentionally align assignments and assessments to the appropriate level of rigor. The precise use of verbs is essential to ensure reliable prompts and output from AI tools.

FIGURE 6.2 EXAMPLE OF STANDARD, GOAL, AND TASK ALIGNMENT FOR AN ASSIGNMENT

Standard: Read closely to determine what a text says explicitly and to make logical inferences from it; cite specific textual evidence to support conclusions drawn from the text.	
The Assignment: Read the essay posted in the course management system and answer the comprehension questions.	
Standards-Aligned, Scaffolded Learning Goal	**Learning-Goal-Aligned Question or Task**
Students will identify specific textual evidence to support what the text says explicitly.	What are three pieces of evidence the author provides to support the claim that the agricultural revolution was "history's biggest fraud"?
Students will make claims about inferences they've drawn from a text and justify those inferences by citing specific, relevant textual evidence.	Is the author's accounting of events objective? State your position as a claim, justify it by citing specific, relevant textual evidence, and then explain your reasoning.

Derive Learning Goals from Standards, Then Use Them to Design Tasks

A *learning goal* is a statement of the knowledge, understanding, or skill that students are to learn. An *activity* is the task or assignment that students do to develop and demonstrate attainment of the goal (see Figure 6.2). "What is the assignment?" is all a student needs to know to seek compliance. However, to engage in intentional learning, "What is the learning goal?" needs to be known by the teacher (to design quality tasks and plan aligned lessons) and the learner (to inform and monitor the effectiveness of their strategy and effort to attain the goal). Note the distinctions in the rigor of the goals based on the use of the verbs *identify*, *explain*, and *justify* in the learning goals in Figure 6.2.

Use Rubrics to Establish a Shared Understanding of Important Attributes of Quality

In a culture of compliance, rubrics often read like a checklist of required elements or are used as an afterthought to score student work and justify a grade. In a culture of learning, rubrics establish a shared understanding of the most important attributes of quality. As Jay McTighe and I explain, "Well-crafted rubrics can serve as a shared road map for teaching and learning. They mark the most important routes for teachers and students to navigate as they walk the circuitous path to deeper learning and more effective performances" (McTighe & Frontier, 2022). Consider how students might use the rubric in Figure 6.3 to guide learning efforts and ensure they are aligned to learning goals.

FIGURE 6.3 EXAMPLE SUCCESS CRITERIA ALIGNED TO A SCALE FOR RIGOR

Standard: Read closely to determine what a text says explicitly and to make logical inferences from it; cite specific textual evidence to support conclusions drawn from the text.				
Example of a Reliable Scale for Levels of Rigor	**Level 1:** Identify, define, or follow a rote step correctly.	**Level 2:** Identify and describe relevant content or follow procedures correctly.	**Level 3:** Connect, compare, and explain relationships among content and concepts.	**Level 4:** Justify reasoning or transfer skills and understandings to solve authentic open-ended problems.
Standard-Aligned as Rubric to the Scale for Rigor	**Level 1:** Identifies "right there in the text" evidence to answer closed-ended questions about *what, when, where,* and *who.*	**Level 2:** Identifies and describes evidence from the text to answer closed-ended questions about *why* and *how.*	**Level 3:** Draws conclusions and makes logical inferences from the text; supports them by citing specific textual evidence.	**Level 4:** Justifies and explains the relevance and/or logic of one's inferences, or one's use of evidence, to support conclusions drawn from the text.

Ensure Fidelity of Opportunity to Learn

By intentionally aligning standards, success criteria, learning goals, and assessment tasks, we can plan lessons and use intentionally aligned instructional strategies that tend to students' needs to develop competence and expect success. For detailed examples of how to align these elements to specific, research-based instructional strategies that ensure students' opportunity to learn, Robert Marzano's *The Art and Science of Teaching* (2007) is a great place to begin.

Use Feedback in Meaningful Ways

In a culture of learning, feedback has two primary purposes: to objectively explain whether and how the work meets previously articulated success criteria and to guide students' efforts to improve performance. What matters most is how students put that feedback to use; in a culture of learning, students are taught how to use feedback to reassess their learning strategies and to revise their evidence of learning. (See Brookhart, 2017, for more on this topic.)

Action Step 4: Teach Students to Plan, Self-Monitor, and Self-Assess

Metacognition is the process of thinking about our own thinking (Flavell, 1979). It is the voice that says, "Slow down!" when you read words that you don't understand, or that says, "Oh! This is similar to X; now I get it!" when you figure something out. Every learner is metacognitive, but not every learner is *productively* metacognitive. Figure 6.4 shows a series of questions that teachers can ask students to help them intentionally and productively plan, self-monitor, and self-assess throughout the learning process. In a culture of compliance, these prompts may appear odd to teachers. "How will I have time for that?" they may ask. "If they aren't graded, my students won't bother with them." But in a culture of learning, teachers understand that prompts such as these are intrinsically motivating to students. You can seamlessly integrate these prompts across lessons, units, assignments, and assessments. And because they are about the learners' thinking, they cannot simply be plugged into an AI tool to deliver the "right answer."

FIGURE 6.4 PROMPTS TO HELP STUDENTS PLAN, MONITOR, AND ASSESS THEIR LEARNING

Planning	• What are some things you already know about this topic, concept, or skill? • Underline language in the assignment and/or success criteria that is unclear to you. • Given the learning goal(s) and the success criteria, restate the purpose of this assignment in your own words. • What are the steps you'll need to take to successfully complete this assignment? • Describe a strategy you will use to achieve the goal(s) and intentionally complete the assignment. • What will you do if you get stuck?
Self-Monitoring	• What is going well on as you work on this goal or assignment? Why? • What content, concepts, or skills are becoming clearer to you? Explain. • What content, concepts, or skills are confusing to you? What questions do you have about these? • What strategies are working well for you and your learning? Why? • Where are you getting stuck and why? How might you apply the same strategies differently? What are different strategies you might try? Explain your thinking.
Self-Assessment	• Complete this sentence frame: The best part of my work is _____ because _____. • Using the language of the success criteria, someone looking at my work would say _____. • A question I am wondering about now that I've completed this work is _____. • Now that I've accomplished this goal, a strategy that worked well and that I should continue to use is _____. • What did you do that you think most contributed to your efforts to meet the success criteria for this assignment? Explain. • What could I (the teacher) have done to make the learning goal, success criteria, or assignment clearer to you?

Source: Adapted from information in Cambridge International Teaching and Learning Team (2019) and Frontier (2021).

Action Step 5: Emphasize Integrity, Transparency, and Explainability

In Chapter 3, I described the importance of clarifying for students when AI tools should, and should not, be used on different assignments and assessments (see Action Step 3.3). I also provided a series of prompts that students can be asked to ensure their evidence of learning demonstrates *integrity, transparency, and explainability* (see Action Step 3.4). If those elements don't come to mind, take a quick look back at them now. By emphasizing the importance of integrity, transparency, and explainability as essential elements to align our efforts to teach with students' efforts to learn, we can clarify for students that what we value most is learning. This partnership could be communicated in a course syllabus as follows:

> It is important that you submit your own work so I can provide meaningful feedback to you to inform your next efforts to learn. If I don't know what you do or don't know, I can't adjust my instruction to better support your learning. It's okay not to know. It's okay to ask questions. If you knew all this already, there'd be no need for you to take this class.
>
> Academic integrity means you own what you know, acknowledge what you don't know, and are transparent about the ideas or words you use that are drawn from the work of others or generated by AI tools. Sometimes I'll ask you to retrace your steps so I can affirm or assist with the strategy you've used to complete a task. I'll always expect you to cite your sources. I'll always expect you to give credit to others or to a technology tool when credit is due.
>
> Academic dishonesty involves any attempt to take credit for knowledge or skills that you don't actually possess. An inability to explain your work may, or may not, be evidence of academic dishonesty. But it does indicate that you haven't internalized that knowledge or those skills yet. If that is the case, I need to know so I can help you learn.

A statement like this isn't meant to replace a school's academic integrity policy. It is intended to communicate a message to students that our relationship is not antagonistic. The purpose of our work together isn't to monitor and attain compliance. The purpose of our work together is to intentionally align our efforts to effectively teach and learn.

Questions for Reflection and Discussion

1. What is a culture of learning, and how does it differ from a culture of compliance?
2. What are the "twin sins" of curriculum design, and how can using AI tools contribute to committing them?
3. What are some of the resources, values, and strategies common to cultures of learning?
4. What questions can teachers use to design assessments that provide evidence of important learning?
5. What strategies can teachers use to align teaching priorities to students' learning efforts?
6. How can learners benefit from self-monitoring and self-assessing?
7. How can emphasizing integrity, transparency, and explainability minimize issues of academic integrity?
8. How does a culture of learning support effective teaching and learning in an era of ubiquitous access to AI tools?

7

Prompt AI Tools Intentionally
Ensure AI Tools Are Used to Create Clarity for Teaching and Learning

AI tools have an unlimited capacity to produce resources for teaching. *But more is not better.* An overabundance of resources, or resources that aren't well aligned with our priorities, distracts students from prioritizing their efforts to learn. However, when prompted intentionally, AI tools can be used to efficiently and effectively generate quality instructional resources. By framing our use of AI tools as a choice between clutter and clarity, we can ensure that we interact with those tools in ways that support intentional teaching and learning.

Clutter vs. Clarity

Clutter is anything that distracts our students from prioritizing their strategy and effort to learn (Frontier, 2021). In the information age, we are awash in clutter. Way back in 1971, Nobel Prize winner Herbert Simon stated:

> In an information-rich world, the wealth of information means a dearth of something else: a scarcity of whatever it is that information consumes. What information consumes is rather obvious: it consumes the attention of its recipients. Hence, a wealth of information creates a poverty of attention. (p. 40)

Simon couldn't have imagined the vast amount of information available at our fingertips today. Because there are no barriers to entry for posting something online, much of what's available is of low quality. A Google search for "rubrics" and "lesson plans" yields nearly a billion results. Some of these may be useful, but more often than not they don't align to our students' learning goals or background knowledge and abilities.

AI tools aren't too different. Absent a clear purpose for prompting an AI tool, you'll get responses that are no better than randomly selecting the seventh hit on a Google search or the tenth hit on a click-for-pay teacher resource site. To add salt to the wound, the AI tool will say, "Sure, I can help with that!" before politely aiding and abetting the twin sins of integration of AI tools (automaticity or efficiency without fidelity) or of curriculum design (coverage or activities without understanding).

The output of AI tools is only as good as the input. Clarity is a choice we make on behalf of our students to help them prioritize their strategy and effort to learn. Before using AI tools, we have to be clear about our priorities so we can craft intentional prompts that produce useful responses and resources.

Action Steps: Prompt AI Tools Intentionally

To ensure AI tools are used in ways that create clarity for teaching, follow these action steps:

1. Prioritize before prompting.
2. Prompt with purpose when using AI tools to develop resources for teaching.
3. Revise output for fidelity, document for transparency, and ensure explainability.
4. Use AI tools as a fidelity coach.
5. Use AI tools as an empathy coach.

Action Step 1: Prioritize Before Prompting

Before reaching for an AI tool to generate an instructional resource, ask yourself this question: "Does a high-quality resource already exist that is aligned to the relevant learning goals, priority standards, and student needs?" If the answer is yes and you can access the resource, do so. If you are unsure, ask someone in school or district leadership; it's their job to help you. If the answer is no, you'll need to do some pre-planning to use AI tools intentionally.

Before prompting AI tools to develop instructional resources, rubrics, assignments, assessments, performance tasks, unit overviews, etc., you'll need to be clear about 1) your purpose for teaching, 2) your learners and their needs, and 3) the context of when and where the teaching and learning will occur. This can be done by reflecting on, or gathering information related to, answers to questions such as those that follow.

Clarify Your Purpose for Teaching Before Prompting AI Tools

- **Identify priority standards and important content, concepts, and skills.** Before prompting AI tools, know your answers to questions such as *What standards are most important for this unit/lesson/assessment? What important academic content, concepts, and skills will students put forth effort to intentionally learn in this unit/lesson/assessment?*

- **Use a consistent language of rigor for learning goals, assessment tasks, and success criteria.** Before prompting AI tools, know your answers to questions such as *How will you discern among different levels of rigor by using precise verbs* (identify, describe, explain, synthesize, analyze, *etc.*) *or descriptive language* (relevant, clear, well-aligned, detailed, *etc.*) *to describe important attributes of quality assessment evidence?*

- **Match assessment methods to types of learning goals.** Before prompting AI tools, know your answers to questions such as *What assessment methods (multiple choice, short answer, extended response, essay, performance task) are best aligned to the standards and learning goals? How will the evidence demonstrate important understandings rather than surface-level coverage or compliance with activities?*

Be Clear About Your Learners and Their Needs Before Prompting AI Tools

- **Identify relevant information about your students and their needs.** Before prompting AI tools, know your answers to questions such as *What is the grade level of the students being taught? What relevant background knowledge and skills do students have? Are there instructional resources that should be differentiated to ensure appropriate levels of challenge and support? How will students be given opportunities to plan, reflect on, and self-assess their work?*

Be Clear About Your Context Before Prompting AI Tools

- **Determine how the resource or tool fits into a lesson, unit, or course.** Before prompting AI tools, know your answers to questions such as *Where does this lesson/unit/resource/assessment fit into the overall sequence of students' learning experiences in this course? Are students acquiring new content, making meaning, or transferring knowledge and skills to authentic contexts? Is the resource to be used formatively or summatively? Independently or in groups? How much instructional time will be allocated for this task/lesson/unit?*

- **Determine boundaries for what resources or tools should or should not be used.** Before prompting AI tools, know your answers to questions such as *What specific resources will all students have access to? Are there resources students should not use (e.g., do not require outside research, the use of scientific calculators)? Or resources or tools that should be used (e.g., require the use of a protractor, students must cite all sources in APA style)?*

Once you are clear about your 1) purpose for teaching, 2) your learners and their needs, and 3) the context when and where the learning will occur, you are ready to prompt AI tools with the intentionality required to ensure clarity.

Action Step 2: Prompt with Purpose

Now that you've gathered or determined information related to your intentions for teaching, you can apply that information and aligned resources in ways that ensure the AI tool's output is reliably aligned to your priorities. To prompt AI tools with purpose, follow these steps.

1. Pre-assess the AI tool.
2. Provide the tool with information about your purpose, learners, and context.
3. Provide instructions and examples.
4. Be specific.
5. Establish process and product constraints.
6. Provide feedback to the AI tool.
7. Refine and revise prompts as needed.

Pre-assess the AI tool

Before collaborating with an AI tool to create resources for teaching or learning, pre-assess the tool to find out what it knows about the topic at hand. The more you know about the topic yourself, the better you'll be able to discern the tool's reliability. If the topic is new to you, spend time with human-created sources to ensure the AI tool isn't hallucinating. Here are some examples of pre-assessment prompts you could use:

- *Are you familiar with Harper Lee's novel* To Kill a Mockingbird? *If so, please provide a short summary of the novel and a short description of each of the main characters.*
- *What do you know about Biggs and Colis's SOLO framework? Please provide a short summary of each level of the framework and examples of learning goals aligned to each level.*
- *Have you been trained on, or can you access, the Next Generation Science Standards (NGSS)? If so, please provide a short overview of the standards' science and engineering practices, cross-cutting concepts, and disciplinary core ideas.*
- *I've attached an article titled "The Fall of the Roman Empire." Provide a one-paragraph summary of the article and a brief outline of the author's claims and supporting evidence.*

Note the form and function of these example prompts. If you just ask the initial question, most AI tools will produce long summaries or explanations. It is better to immediately follow the query with a task designed to help you ascertain the accuracy and quality of the tool's output. If the tool has not been trained on the topic or cannot access the requested information, it will usually tell you.

Provide the Tool with Information About Your Purpose, Learners, and Context

Providing information about your purpose, learners, and context means you tell the AI tool relevant information about who you are, why you are using the tool, and how you will use the output it produces. Here are two examples; notice that while both focus on the same academic content, the specific information about the purpose, learners, and context will produce very different types of responses from the AI tool:

- I am a 5th grade teacher in a rural elementary school. Most of the students in my classroom are English speakers, but several are Spanish speakers or bilingual in Spanish and English. I'd like to prepare some grade-appropriate definitions, explanations, and real-world examples of the eight science practices in the NGSS standards.
- I teach a capstone science course at a college-prep academy for high-achieving high school seniors. I'd like to develop some ideas for authentic performance tasks that students can complete in small groups across a period of three weeks at the end of the school year. The ideas for tasks should require students to intentionally apply each of the eight science practices described in the NGSS standards.

Provide Instructions and Give Examples

Effective prompting is often about giving commands rather than just asking questions. Be directive; tell the tool exactly what you want it to do. The reliability of the output can be improved by providing specific examples of the type of output you want the tool to generate. The number of examples (or, in AI parlance, *shots*) you provide can improve the reliability of the output with a shorter prompt, but it can take more time to develop. Consider the following:

- **Example of a Zero-Shot Prompt:** Provide a brief, grade-appropriate explanation and example of each of the eight NGSS science practices for a 5th grade class. Each explanation and example should be provided in English and Spanish.
- **Example of a One-Shot Prompt:** A one-shot prompt provides a single example for the AI tool to use as a model when generating output. Provide a brief, grade-appropriate explanation of each of the eight NGSS science practices including a real-life example following this format:

  Science and Engineering Practice: Analyzing and interpreting data

  Explanation: Scientists observe the world around them and record what they see using pictures, words, or numbers. *Analyzing* means to look for patterns or relationships. *Interpret* means to explain what patterns or relationships exist. *Data* is a word scientists use to describe, or count, what they see.

Example: A student wants to know what type of soil is the best to use for growing grass. The student plants three grass seeds each in three different types of soil. Each type of soil receives the same amount of sunlight and water. After a week, the student measures the grass and records the average length of the grasses in each type of soil as 38mm, 32mm, and 25mm (*the data*). The student reports that the longest grass came from the first type of soil (*the analysis*). The student concludes that the first type of soil is the best for growing grass (*the interpretation*).

A multiple-shot prompt provides several examples and, therefore, requires fewer commands. However, designing the examples can take time.

Example of a Multiple-Shot Prompt: Provide a brief, grade-appropriate explanation of each of the eight NGSS science practices including a real-life example formatted as in the examples that follow: [Note to reader: You would paste multiple examples here using the same formatting used in the one-shot example above.]

Be Specific

If prompts are too vague, they are likely to generate clutter. For example, prompts such as these are too general to provide useful results:

- Create a unit plan about the Roman Empire.
- Make a rubric for my students' essays on *Romeo and Juliet*.
- Generate three projects my students can do about the water cycle.

Instead, be as specific as possible with your prompts, drawing on relevant elements related to your purpose for teaching, your learners, and the context of where and when learning will occur as in this example:

My 5th grade students are learning about the water cycle. They are to meet the following NGSS performance indicator: "Develop a model to describe the cycling of water through Earth's systems driven by energy from the sun and the force of gravity." Important academic vocabulary words from the unit include *evaporation, condensation, precipitation, transpiration, runoff,* and *collection.* The cross-cutting concepts central to the unit are "cause and effect" and "stability and change." The science and engineering practices central to the unit are "develops and uses models" and "constructs explanations."

Follow these instructions:

- Create a unit plan that can be completed in ten 50-minute lessons.
- The unit should begin with an activity that allows me to pre-assess each student's initial level of knowledge and skills in a low-stakes manner.
- Each lesson should end with an exit ticket that can be completed in two minutes or less and helps me monitor students' understanding of content.
- A sample unit planning template has been uploaded for you to emulate in terms of tone, verbiage, and format.
- The success criteria scales for the performance indicators "Develops and Uses Models" and "Constructs Explanations" have been uploaded. These scales will be used to plan, scaffold, and assess students' learning as they progress through the unit. Learning goals, assessment prompts, and evidence of understanding should be aligned to and reference these scales.
- The culminating assessment should provide evidence that allows me to make valid and reliable inferences about the indicators "Develops and Uses Models" and "Constructs Explanations" using the provided scales.

The response will not be perfect. But it will provide a starting point that is based on your priorities for teaching and students' learning.

Establish Process and Product Constraints

To design effective prompts, do as engineers do and *articulate constraints*: establish the boundaries that clarify what a process or product must and must not include. When using an AI tool to create learning or teaching resources, a process constraint is any such boundary related to the learning process. Here are a few examples that could be included in prompts:

- The unit needs to be taught over fifteen 48-minute class periods.
- Students must focus on the following standards and success criteria in their learning efforts: [teacher uploads standards and criteria].

- Students should receive feedback on their initial formative work and be required to explain any modifications they make to their work due to the feedback.
- Unit content should be introduced in the same order as shown in the attached document: [teacher uploads a content vocabulary list or unit overview].
- The end-of-unit assessment must provide evidence of whether students have met priority standards. It should also require students to use some of the formative tools they developed during the unit (e.g., graphic organizers, write-ups from investigations), but students should not need anything more than pencil and paper to complete the assessment.

In contrast to a process constraint, a product constraint is anything related to what must or must not be included in the actual AI-generated product. Here are some examples that could be included in prompts:

- Any project options generated for performance tasks must require students to produce evidence of the standards and success criteria pasted below.
- The unit must include each of the elements in the following exemplar unit: [teacher uploads exemplar unit].
- Output should not exceed 500 words and should be written at a 6th grade level. Here are three examples: [teacher uploads examples].
- The 20 multiple-choice questions must be aligned to the standards, the vocabulary list, and the notes I've uploaded. Each question should have five answer options. Ten of the questions should allow for an inference about students' ability to define terms, five should allow for an inference about students' ability to draw meaningful inferences, and another five should allow for an inference about students' ability to support claims with reliable evidence.
- The assessment must include three short-answer prompts that require students to demonstrate their understanding of important knowledge and skills at level 3 of the SOLO framework (relational) as aligned to the attached unit overview.
- Create exemplar and non-exemplar samples of student responses to the following prompt: [teacher pastes prompt here, using brackets or

the return key to set it apart from the other text]. Each sample should be aligned to the success criteria in the attached rubric. The quality of the evidence in the exemplars should be aligned to the descriptors in levels 3 and 4 of the success criteria, and the quality of the evidence in the non-exemplars should be aligned to the descriptors in levels 1 and 2 of the success criteria. Each of the sample responses should be approximately 200 words and read as though written by a 9th grader. For each of the samples, annotate how the evidence is aligned to the corresponding success criteria.

- Rubric descriptors must be aligned to the precise language of the standards provided. Do not include vague descriptors such as *creative* or *interesting*. Do not use vague qualifiers such as *"not very, somewhat, very"* or *"good, great, exceptional."*

You'll note that some of these prompts are very detailed. These details ensure the reliability and usefulness of the output to support your intentions for teaching.

Provide Feedback to the AI Tool

AI tools are designed for meaningful two-way communication. To improve their output, engage them in dialogue and provide them with feedback, such as by affirming that it's generating the output you want or by specifying ways in which the output doesn't meet your criteria. Sometimes it is useful to ask the tool to summarize the instructions you've provided in the prompt or to tell it to annotate how the output provided matches specified criteria. You can also use a "chain of thought" approach, whereby you coach the tool to provide the output you want using incremental steps. Once you are confident that the tool "understands" your request, further hone the output with prompts such as "try again adding . . ." or "regenerate the output but omit. . . ."

Here are some examples of useful feedback to use with AI tools:

- What you've generated is perfect! Now apply that same format for the next topic: [teacher specifies topic]
- The output you've provided is too complex for my students. Continue to use the specific academic language I requested, but the other text should use shorter words and sentences. Try again.

> • The suggestions for student projects you've provided won't require students to develop or demonstrate an understanding of the standards and success criteria I shared. They meet the criteria of being hands-on and engaging, but they need to be more clearly aligned to the priority standards. Regenerate your response. This time, annotate each project showing how it is aligned to specific elements of the priority standards.

Refine and Revise Prompts as Needed

Despite our best attempts, AI tools will sometimes generate responses that are completely off the mark. When this occurs, consider the following strategies:

- Break the prompt into smaller pieces. When you start a new chat with an AI tool, the tool keeps track of the criteria and feedback throughout that session. So, rather than giving a long prompt, engage the tool one step at a time. For example: "Now that you've accomplished that successfully, I'd like to take what you've generated and move on to the next step. Based on that output above, provide...."
- Use sentence starters. For example: "Each of the learning goals should be framed as an 'I can' statement. Generate the learning goals again, but this time be sure they are explicitly aligned to the standards. Use 'I can' to start each learning goal."
- Use symbols to indicate formatting that should not be changed and let the tool know what they represent. For example: "Phrases between the asterisks in the template, such as *Level 1 and Level 2* or *Essential Questions and Enduring Understandings*, should not be modified."
- Clear the cache. Amidst long sequences of prompts, AI tools can glitch. Simply type, "Start a new chat."
- Ask yourself whether the tool is right for the job. Try the task again without using the tool.

AI tools aren't magic. They use layers of mathematical code to predict the word or pixel that is most likely to come next. By prompting with purpose, you can increase the likelihood that the output you receive is aligned to your priorities for teaching.

Action Step 3: Revise for Fidelity, Document for Transparency, and Ensure Explainability

Teachers should consider anything an AI tool generates to be a draft rather than a final version. Consider asking yourself these questions about any output to guide revisions to ensure fidelity, document for transparency, and ensure explainability.

Questions About Revising for Fidelity

- Is its output aligned to priority standards and content?
- Is it rooted in the vocabulary, learning opportunities, and resources that are the focus of this unit?
- Is it free of bias, inaccuracies, and errors?
- Does it help students align their efforts to learn the most important unit content, concepts, and skills?
- If students do the AI-generated task/project/assignment/assessment, will it yield evidence of students' independent understanding of the most important standards and learning goals?

Questions About Documenting for Transparency

Have I transparently documented . . .

- My efforts to clarify the purpose of this product and its alignment to priorities for intentional teaching and students' learning needs?
- Both the prompts and responses from the AI tool?
- Any revisions I made to the output before using it?
- How I ensured the accuracy and reliability of an AI automated process?
- Have I cited or referenced my use of AI tools?

Questions to Ensure Explainability

Can I explain to students and colleagues . . .

- How the choices I made when prompting the AI tool were based on my purpose and students' learning priorities?
- The meaning of academic language, content, success criteria, or feedback articulated by the AI tool?
- How to apply the skills, steps, or procedures articulated by the AI tool?

Can I explain and justify to colleagues and administrators . . .

- How the output aligns to my purpose for teaching and my students' priorities for learning?
- How the output from the AI tool is well aligned to, or differs from, school-, district-, or state-provided resources?
- How the marks, feedback, or grades that were the result of students' use of an AI-generated task, assessment, or rubric are valid and reliable?

By considering any initial AI output as a draft, we can take steps to ensure it has fidelity to our priorities for teaching and our students' learning needs. By transparently documenting and reporting how we've used AI tools, we can model the intentionality and integrity we expect of our students. Finally, by ensuring we can explain any AI-related output, we build trust in others that we've applied our professional expertise to use AI with intention.

Action Step 4: Use AI as a Fidelity Coach

AI tools can serve as a fidelity coach or a critical friend. You can request feedback from AI tools on the alignment of standards, success criteria, assessments, and unit plans. In the following example, I submitted a multiple-choice assessment from a U.S. history course that I'd identified as heavy on trivia and light on both rigor and substance. The assessment is typical of those used in classrooms focused on "coverage without understanding." I uploaded the assessment into an AI tool and provided the following prompt:

> I teach a 10th grade U.S. history course. In the attached document, I've included the five academic content standards and the two historical inquiry standards that were used to design the 30-item assessment. Your task is to do the following: 1) review the standards, 2) review the assessment, and 3) provide me with a critique of whether and how the assessment is aligned to the standards.

And here's how the AI tool (ChatGPT 4.0) responded:

Rigor and Historical Inquiry Standards
- Matching and Multiple-Choice Format: These are appropriate for assessing factual knowledge but may not fully engage higher-order thinking skills like analysis and evaluation.
- Historical Inquiry Standard 1: The test could include more questions that require students to connect specific events to "broader social, economic, and political trends."
- Historical Inquiry Standard 2: The test could incorporate more complex cause-and-effect questions, perhaps in a short answer or essay format, to better assess students' abilities to "analyze historical causes and effects."

Suggestions for Improvement

- Diversify question formats: Incorporating short-answer or essay questions could provide opportunities for students to demonstrate higher-level thinking, such as "analyzing and evaluating historical events and their impacts."
- Incorporate more elements on content standards 3, 4, and 5: Expanding the scope of questions to include more about "individuals (e.g., citizens, soldiers), Roosevelt's specific policies, and the broader impact of the war on various groups in the U.S." would enhance alignment with these content standards.
- Connect events to broader trends: Questions that require students to explain how specific events (e.g., battles, policies) "influenced or were the result of larger historical trends" would align well with the historical inquiry standards.

Overall, your assessment covers a range of important content in World War II history. Enhancing it with questions that require deeper analysis and a broader range of question types could increase its rigor and alignment with the stated standards.

For the next example, I intentionally selected a performance assessment from a middle school physics unit that I used as a non-exemplar in my 2021 book *Teaching with Clarity*. Though it is engaging and hands-on, it is also an example of an activity without understanding. The poorly designed assessment emphasizes following directions and earning points over a deep understanding of content as articulated in the success criteria.

To ask the AI tool to critique the assessment, I uploaded the assessment and the grading rubric and provided the following prompt:

Prompt: I teach an 8th-grade science course. I've attached the standards, performance assessment, and grading rubric for a physics unit that requires students to explain scientific principles related to force, motion, mass, friction, and energy as related to simple machines by building a Rube Goldberg device. Please provide a detailed critique of the performance assessment and grading rubric that assesses their fidelity to the specific language of the standards.

And here's how the AI tool responded:

Direct Application of Standards

- The grading criteria mainly focus on assembling the specific components (levers and ramps) and the duration of the device's operation.
- This approach might not fully capture the depth of understanding described in, or application of, the standards, particularly in terms of modeling unobservable mechanisms and constructing scientific explanations related to the structure and function of simple machines as related to force, motion, mass, friction, and energy.

Suggestions for Improvement

- Add a requirement for students to submit a written or oral explanation of their device, detailing how it demonstrates the principles of force, motion, energy, etc. This aligns with the standard of constructing explanations supported by scientific principles.
- Add a requirement for students to include diagrams or labels to illustrate and explain the unobservable mechanisms at play in their device.

Overall Critique

- While the current assessment and grading rubric are engaging and practical, they can be enhanced to ensure evidence of a comprehensive and deep understanding of the scientific principles outlined in the standards.
- By integrating additional criteria that focus on the form and function of simple machines, the characteristics of well-written scientific explanations, and the use of models to describe and demonstrate understanding of unseen forces, the assessment will be more aligned with the specific language and objectives of the standards.

The critique provided by the AI tool for both the U.S. history and the physics examples are both spot on. This feedback from the "fidelity coach" could be used by a teacher to significantly improve the alignment of the assessment to the prioritized standards.

Here are some other examples of potential "fidelity coach" prompts:

- **For a rubric:** I've created the following rubric to assess my 9th grade writing students. The rubric has been arranged using the SOLO framework. I've attached the relevant academic standards for this rubric. Please review the academic standards I've provided and then submit a bulleted critique of the rubric's alignment or misalignment to the standards as well as any recommendations you'd make to ensure alignment.

- **For a unit of instruction:** I've created a two-week unit that will serve as an introduction to inferential statistics as compared to descriptive statistics for my 10th grade statistics course. I've attached the relevant standards, academic vocabulary, disciplinary concepts, and mathematical procedures that are important for my students to learn in this unit. Please review the standards, the academic vocabulary, the disciplinary concepts, and mathematical procedures I've provided in my unit plan. Then, provide a detailed critique of the alignment or misalignment of the unit plan to the standards and any recommendations you'd make to ensure alignment between my stated priorities and learning opportunities the unit provides.

I've been consistently impressed by how adept AI tools can be at analyzing resources and providing meaningful, valid feedback. The key is intentionality.

Another interesting note. I've uploaded teaching resources I'd created and used in the past and found myself completely open to the AI tools' feedback. These are resources that I hadn't ever considered sharing with a colleague and requesting feedback. As I reflect on that, perhaps it's because I didn't want to bother them. Or, if I'm being honest, perhaps it's because I didn't want to be in the vulnerable position of having my work judged by a colleague. There are a lot of possibilities here—for teachers and for students—to use AI tools to improve the quality of our work without having to reveal the limits of our competence to others.

Action Step 5: Use AI as an Empathy Coach

AI tools can be used to more intentionally stand in the shoes of our students and see our classrooms with greater empathy. For example, AI tools can help us understand misconceptions students may have on a topic, provide feedback related to the cognitive load of tasks, and synthesize students' responses to understand their background knowledge. Following are some examples of prompts used for these purposes that can be tailored to different content areas, as well as the responses to the prompts that the AI tool generated.

Example 1: Receive Feedback on Student Misconceptions About Content

Prompt: I am a middle school teacher. Next week my students will begin a unit where they are required to develop and use a model of the Earth-sun-moon system to describe the cyclic patterns of lunar phases. What are some common misconceptions that students have about the Earth-sun-moon system and the cyclic patterns of lunar phases?

AI Tool Response: Teaching about the Earth-sun-moon system and the cyclic patterns of lunar phases can be a fascinating topic for middle school students, but it's also an area where many misconceptions can arise. Here are some common ones:

- *Phases of the moon are caused by Earth's shadow:* Many students mistakenly believe that the lunar phases are caused by Earth's shadow falling on the moon. In reality, lunar phases are due to the changing positions of the Earth, moon, and sun, and how we see the illuminated part of the moon from Earth.
- *The moon has a permanent dark side:* Students might think that one side of the moon is always dark. However, both sides of the moon experience day and night, just like Earth.
- *Eclipses occur every month:* Since new moons and full moons happen monthly, students might think eclipses also happen monthly. However, eclipses only occur when the Earth, sun, and moon are precisely aligned, which doesn't happen every month due to the moon's orbital inclination.
- *The sun orbits the Earth:* Some younger students might still hold a geocentric view of the solar system, believing that the sun orbits the Earth.

It's important to use models, diagrams, and hands-on activities to visually and physically demonstrate these concepts. Doing so can help students better understand the actual mechanics of the Earth-sun-moon system and the reasons behind the observable patterns in lunar phases.

Example 2: Receive Feedback on Cognitive Load

Prompt: I am designing a performance assessment for 9th grade students aligned to the following history standards: [teacher lists standards]. I'd like your feedback on the design of this performance assessment task that I've uploaded. Specifically, I'd like you to provide feedback and recommendations about how to design the task in a manner that minimizes cognitive load for students.

AI Tool Response: Your performance assessment designed for 9th grade students in history is comprehensive and ambitious. It aims to integrate historical analysis, essay writing, presentation skills, and multimedia usage. Here are some recommendations to minimize cognitive load:

- Scaffold the research process. Provide a guided framework for research to help students identify and analyze primary sources effectively.
- Break down the task. Introduce the essay and presentation components in stages and across multiple days of instruction, allowing students to focus on one aspect at a time and receive feedback.
- Provide templates and examples: Offer an essay outline and a slideshow template to guide students in organizing their thoughts and presentations.
- The requirement of "five different high-quality sources" is good for depth but might be overwhelming for 9th graders in terms of research skills. At a minimum, consider providing guidance to clarify what you mean by a "high-quality" source or a list of potential sources.
- Clarify APA style requirements. Since APA style might be new to 9th graders, provide clear guidelines or a simplified version of the APA Manual tailored to their level.

By refining the assessment design with these recommendations, you can enhance its effectiveness and ensure it aligns more closely with the intended learning outcomes.

Example 3: Using AI Tools to Quickly Analyze Formative Assessment Results

Another strategy for using AI tools to empathize with students is to give students open-ended questions, feed their responses to an AI tool, and prompt it to summarize, synthesize, and analyze patterns in their responses.

Design your questions around a focal point (e.g., an equation, a photograph, a short passage of text) that can be used to activate students' background knowledge. Then, design a few questions that intentionally scaffold students to share basic observations and then make more complex inferences in Google Forms or a survey tool. Here are some examples of open-ended questions that can be asked of students:

- *Math*: "Look at the linear equation below. Using precise mathematical language, explain in as much detail as possible what the different parts of the equation represent. Then, in a short paragraph, provide an example to explain how linear equations are used in the real world."
- *History*: "Look at the artwork in this photograph by Faith Ringgold titled 'The Sunflower Quilting Bee at Arles.' What do you see that captures your attention? When do you think the photograph was taken? What do you think the artist is trying to convey in this image and why? What questions do you have about the artist or the subjects or objects in the painting?"

And here is a template you can use to prompt the AI tool's analysis:

I am [a(n) X] grade teacher and my students are learning about [topic]. Specifically, they are starting to develop an understanding of [standard or goal]. After a brief introductory lesson to start the unit, I shared the attached [focal point] with my students and asked them the following questions [upload the focal point and questions]. [Here, provide as much detail as necessary about the focal point or ask the AI tool what it knows about it.] I'd like you to review the attached responses to each question and do the following:

1. Summarize the students' responses to each prompt and answer these questions:

   - What accurate conceptualizations do students hold?
   - What misconceptions or oversimplifications do students have?

> - How precise and accurate is students' academic vocabulary? Provide examples of both specific and vague vocabulary.
> - What background knowledge do students have about the topic that could support their learning? Provide specific examples.
> - What background knowledge are students missing that could inhibit their learning? Provide specific examples.

To engage in this formative assessment strategy without an AI tool would require a few hours at the end of the school day for the teacher to synthesize the responses of 150 students. With the AI tool, detailed insights about students' misconceptions, their more accurate understandings, and their ability to use academic vocabulary accurately can be provided to the teacher in a matter of moments. This is an example of an efficient use of an AI tool that can improve teacher effectiveness. The synthesis presented by the AI tool can be used by the teacher to inform instruction in ways that are intentionally aligned to address students' learning needs.

Questions for Reflection and Discussion

1. What is clutter and how does it undermine effective teaching and learning? How might AI tools exacerbate the challenge of clutter?
2. What is clarity and how does it support effective teaching and learning?
3. Why is it essential to be clear about your purpose for teaching before prompting AI tools to generate instructional resources?
4. How do the example prompts in this chapter draw on principles of fidelity, empathy, and a shared purpose for learning discussed in previous chapters?
5. How does prompting with clear intentions for teaching and learning ensure that output from AI tools is effectively aligned to priorities for teaching and learning?
6. What does it mean to review and revise for fidelity? Document for transparency? Ensure explainability? Who benefits from these steps?
7. How does using AI tools as fidelity coaches demonstrate a transformational use of AI tools?
8. How does using AI tools as empathy coaches demonstrate a transformational use of AI tools?

Empower Students to Use AI Tools Intentionally
Teach Students to Use AI Tools with Agency for Learning

Look at the mission statement or strategic plan of almost any school, and you'll see a reference to some version of "lifelong learners," "student-centered" strategies, or "preparing students for the future." These are important, worthy ideals to pursue. But there is often a gap between the ideals we espouse for our students and the day-to-day realities of schooling. As Nancy Frey, John Hattie, and Doug Fisher (2018) argue:

> Too many students are adult-dependent learners. Others are compliant learners. Neither will serve our society well. What we need are learners who understand their current performance, recognize the gap between their current performance and the expected performance, and select strategies to close that gap. (Frey et al. 2018, p. 6)

If students see AI as little more than an "answer engine" to easily comply with assigned tasks, tomorrow's students will be adult- *and* AI-dependent learners who are even less prepared for the future. AI tools have unlimited capacity to be used by students as tools for active, intentional learning. If we want them to use them in these ways, they'll need to be taught how.

Dependent vs. Independent Learners

A dependent learner is a passive recipient of information and teaching (Meyer et al., 2008). These students see school as a series of day-to-day-to-do lists that begin and end with the teacher. *The teacher assigns work, I do it as best I can, turn it in, and the teacher assigns a grade.* Dependent students lack agency; they don't believe they are capable of exerting any control over their learning environment. If they aren't told to do it, it doesn't exist.

An independent learner invests strategy and effort to actively direct and regulate their own learning (Meyer et al., 2008). These students have a strong sense of *agency*; they take intentional action to exert control over their learning environment (Bandura, 2006). They believe their role is to actively plan, monitor, and adapt their strategies to pursue goals for learning. Figure 8.1 shows some of the key differences between dependent and independent learners.

Dependence or Independence? Applying Strategies to a Resource

Imagine a re-prioritization of global resources that makes it possible for every child in grades 6-12 to have his or her own tutor for each of their courses. Consider the following scenarios and the questions that follow:

> **Tutor Scenario 1:** *The tutors are required to answer any questions and do any tasks, including any homework or projects, that are assigned to the student. The student simply needs to ask the tutor to do the work. Would students use this resource? If so, what would be the long-term result?*

FIGURE 8.1 CHARACTERISTICS OF DEPENDENT VS. INDEPENDENT LEARNERS

Dependent Learners	Resource	Independent Learners
Primarily focused on rewards or consequences (extrinsic)	**Goals**	Primarily focused on learning (intrinsic)
See assessment as summative and meant to punish or reward	**Assessment**	See assessment as formative and meant to affirm or inform learning efforts
Seek "the answer" (but avoid both help and struggle)	**Assistance**	Monitor understanding, persevere, and seek help when needed
Seek praise for what they *did* or ignore feedback altogether	**Feedback**	Seek and apply meaningful feedback about how they are *doing*
Passively receive academic content	**Agency**	Persistently and assertively influence conditions to help make sense of academic content
Monitor compliance with requirements or directions	**Self-Monitoring**	Apply, monitor, and reflect on the effectiveness of strategy and effort to learn

Tutor Scenario 2: *The tutors will not answer any teacher-assigned questions, complete any teacher-assigned tasks, nor correct students' responses to any teacher-assigned tasks. The tutor will help the student pursue learning goals but only by responding to the student's own questions or requests. Would students use this resource? If so, what would be the long-term result?*

When I share these tutoring scenarios as sequential slides in workshops, teachers recognize that by replacing "tutors" with "AI tools", these choices aren't hypothetical.

Scenario 1 is typically greeted with a chorus of "That's what they do!" followed by groans and patter about AI, shortcuts, and cheating. There's agreement that students would use these tutors as a task-rabbit to do their work for them, but they'd learn less and become increasingly dependent on the tutor.

Scenario 2 is typically greeted with nervous silence. Teachers agree that a few naturally curious students would choose this tutor, but most students wouldn't have any idea where to even start. At that point, someone points out that those who would benefit the most from these tutors would be the least likely to know how to ask for help.

The reason I frame this thought exercise as being about tutors rather than AI tools is because it prevents us from diagnosing and dismissing AI as the problem. Instead, we can take a more empathetic approach. Whether students are entirely dependent on their teacher, a tutor, or an AI tool to do their work, the result is the same; students learn less and become increasingly dependent. It's not that these resources *can't* be used for learning. Maybe the students aren't interested in working with the second group of tutors because students see compliance, rather than learning, as the purpose of school. Or, maybe it's because students have become so dependent on their teachers that, as workshop participants often identify, they wouldn't have any idea where to even start.

Student Agency and Schooling

As I have small groups discuss these tutoring scenarios, I often hear a few teachers saying, "But *what are* the students supposed to do with the second group of tutors?" Let's reframe that question by asking a slightly different question that I discussed in a recent *Educational Leadership* article (Frontier, 2025): What does a highly agentic learner look like in the classroom? Consider the answer from researchers Johnmarshall Reeve and Ching-Mei Tseng:

During the flow of instruction, students might offer input, express a preference, offer a suggestion or contribution, ask a question, communicate what they are thinking and needing, recommend a goal or objective to be pursued . . . seek ways to add personal relevance, ask for a say in how problems are to be solved, seek clarification . . . communicate likes and dislikes, or request assistance such as modeling, tutoring, feedback, background knowledge, or a concrete example of an abstract concept. (Reeve & Tseng, 2011, p. 258)

As any kindergarten teacher who reads this quote can tell you, students arrive to school bursting with agency. But as any teacher who reads this quote can also tell you, an entire classroom of students seeking—or even demanding—this level of agency and independence at all times would be impossible to teach. Out of logistical necessity, students are taught that some passive compliance is necessary to make schooling possible.

As much as we lament students whose only questions seem to be "How many points is this worth?" and "Can't you just tell me the answer?" we have to acknowledge that they didn't arrive at school that way. If students conclude that there isn't much they can do to exert control over their learning environment, they'll make the logical but debilitating choice to trade agency for learning with efficiency for schooling.

Dependence vs. Independence: The Role of the Teacher

One way for teachers to support students' independence is by taking an autonomy-supportive approach to teaching (Reeve & Cheon, 2021; Reeve & Shin, 2020). This approach "adopts the students' perspective, asks students what they want and prefer, and incorporates students' input and suggestions into the ongoing flow of instruction" (Reeve & Shin, 2020, p. 153). Autonomy-supportive practices intrinsically motivate students to pursue rigorous goals for learning by balancing their need for autonomy with their need for competence.

The autonomy-supportive approach to teaching contrasts with three other approaches—controlling, neutral, and laissez-faire:

- In a *controlling approach*, the teacher dictates what and how "students should think, feel, and do" (p. 153).

- In an *indifferent approach*, the teacher tends to be indifferent to students' "needs, goals, and concerns" (p. 154). The teacher presents content and gives assignments but is largely unresponsive to students' needs.
- In a *laissez-faire approach*, the teacher largely leaves students on their own to assume responsibility and take the initiative to learn. The teacher provides endless autonomy but fails to be autonomy-*supportive* in ways that provide intentional opportunities for students to build their competence.

For an adult-dependent student working with a controlling or indifferent teacher in a culture of compliance, they've already internalized a set of strategies to effectively "do school." When these students are given a resource—whether it is a book, a tutor, or an AI tool—the conditioned response is to use the resource to answer the teacher's questions to gain compliance.

For a student working with a teacher who uses a laissez-faire approach, students may be more likely to see AI as a tool that can level the playing field because they haven't had the opportunity to learn what is being asked of them. Generative AI tools are well-suited to deliver definitive responses to seemingly random questions and ambiguous tasks.

When generative AI tools became widely available in 2022, students didn't have to learn how to use them to gain compliance; they simply applied the skills and strategies they'd honed over the years to passively comply in the past even more efficiently. If students aren't taught how to apply strategies that support agency and independence, they'll engage with resources—whether those resources are classmates, teachers, tutors, Google, or AI tools—to ask superficial questions that provide the path of least resistance to getting the answer. Autonomy-supportive practices that build agency and independence can inoculate students from this debilitating approach.

How AI Tools Can Be Used to Support Student Agency and Build Independence

What I find remarkable about the lengthy quote from Reeve and Tseng (2011) I'd shared earlier in this chapter is that they describe the types of prompts and chats that generative AI tools excel at. When prompted intentionally by students, AI tools can be a non-judgmental, endlessly patient resource, tutor, or thought partner. What matters is how these tools are used. Recent anecdotal and academic research supports these claims. For example I've argued (Frontier, 2025) that:

- **AI tools can be used in ways that are immediately responsive to and supportive of highly agentic students.** Secondary teacher Jack Dougall (2023) gave his students a performance task and told them they could complete it using AI any way they wanted. Most students compliantly asked the AI tool for the answers, and regardless of whether or not they understood the output, they dutifully replicated those answers and turned them in. But, there was a small group of students who took a more active, agentic approach. According to Dougall, these students were "the rogue learners, the questioners, the bickerers, the challengers. . . . They 'chatted' with the AI, questioned it, and they argued with it. They fine-tuned their prompts and engaged in a back-and-forth with the AI" (2023). This group of students became so engaged in the task that they clamored for more time to write down all they'd learned. On an assessment given after the task was complete, the agentic, "rogue" learners outperformed their compliant classmates. The agentic strategies they used to support their learning were perfectly aligned to the capacity of the transformational tool.

- **When prompted intentionally, AI tools can support students' needs for competence**. In studies that show increased student learning as a result of using AI (Baillifard et al., 2025; Bastani et al., 2024; Kestin et al., 2024; Kumar et al., 2023), the AI tool had been prompted to respond in ways that are aligned with students' needs for competence. Specifically, the AI tools were prompted to:
  - Check for understanding before providing new information.
  - *Not* tell students the answers to any questions or tasks until students attempt them first.
  - Ask clarifying questions before moving on.
  - Limit the length of responses to ensure they don't overwhelm students.

- **When prompted intentionally, AI tools can support students' needs for autonomy**. Using a pre-test/post-test design, undergraduate physics students learned twice as much—in less time—using an AI tutor than in a whole-group, interactive lesson (Kestin et al., 2024). The AI tool was fine-tuned to adhere to the competency-supportive constraints described above. Not only did the AI-tutored students learn more, but they also reported higher levels of engagement and motivation. Why? The authors noted that students could spend as much—or as little—time as necessary in the module, ask and receive immediate answers to clarifying questions, and receive and respond to personalized feedback in real time.

There are two important take-aways from these findings. First, when used intentionally, students can use AI tools to support their learning rather than just to complete tasks. Second, when used intentionally, AI tools can be responsive to students' needs for autonomy and competence in ways that are difficult—if not impossible—to provide and support through whole-class instruction.

Six Skills of Independent Learners

Here are six high-leverage skills that independent learners can utilize with the support of AI tools. These skills are time-tested and high-leverage; whether or not they are applied with the support of AI tools they are still worth developing in every learner. However, because students can apply these strategies to AI tools beyond what can be reasonably provided by a single teacher in a single class period, students may find these skills more practical and applicable than ever before. Each of these skills are discussed in the section that follows. Then, in the action steps for this chapter, I'll describe how students can intentionally apply these skills with the support of AI tools. Independent learners:

1. Focus on goals rather than the completion of tasks.
2. Self-assess learning strategies and efforts.
3. Engage in productive struggle and ask for help.
4. Seek and apply feedback to inform learning efforts.
5. Are persistent and assertive.
6. Monitor the effectiveness of their strategy, effort, and results.

Independent Learners Are Goal-Focused

The distinctions between learning and compliance were discussed in detail in previous chapters. Figure 8.2 points out some key distinctions in the questions that learning-goal-focused, as compared to task-focused students, use to guide their effort.

In Chapter 6, Figure 6.2 showed how a standard, assignment, learning goals, and assessment tasks can be aligned to support intentional teaching and learning. A student who is learning-goal-focused will use words such as *identify, infer, justify, support, specific,* and *relevant* in the goals and the tasks to monitor their

FIGURE 8.2 GOAL- VS. TASK-FOCUSED QUESTIONS

Questions That Reveal an Active Learning-Goal Focus	Questions That Reveal a Compliant, Task Focus
• What knowledge or skill-related learning goal am I trying to improve through this assignment? • What do I understand already? • What questions will clarify where I am confused and/or could deepen my understanding? • What are the success criteria, and how can I use them to focus my efforts to produce quality work? • What tools and strategies can I use to deepen my understanding? • How can I use feedback to affirm or inform my next efforts? • What did I learn?	• What is the assignment? • Is this graded and how many total points is it worth? • How many points is each required element/ question worth? • What tools and strategies can I use to successfully complete the assignment with the least amount of effort? • What are the correct answers? • What is my grade?

thinking and their use of strategies to learn. A dependent, compliant learner will be more likely to read the question and search for the answer.

Independent Learners Self-Assess

The quote at the beginning of this chapter about how independent learners use classroom assessment evidence to monitor their progress captures the essence of how independent learners are intentional in their efforts to align strategy and effort. They continuously self-assess to inform their strategy and effort to pursue goals for intentional learning (Black & Wiliam, 1998, 2009; Hattie, 2021).

Independent Learners Struggle and Seek Help

Independent learners see productive struggle and asking for help as valuable parts of the learning process. It is a mistake to assume that students avoid asking for help because they lack motivation (Edmondson & Lei, 2014). Students may avoid asking for help because they fear judgment from others, don't want to slow the teacher's pace, or think the help won't matter (Peeters, 2021). Fortunately, emotionally supportive classroom environments (Ryan et al., 1998), an emphasis on learning from errors (Turner et al. 2002), and actively affirming students' questions (Good & Shaw, 2022), can mitigate some of these challenges. Reducing the risks of asking for help and creating opportunities is not enough. Students need to know *how* to ask for help in ways that are productive. Figure 8.3 shows a variety of ways students may respond when they realize they need help.

Figure 8.4 shows how the task-focused, compliant student only needs to repeatedly ask a single question—"What is the answer?"—to navigate their entire schooling experience. Absent effort and reflection applied to transferable goals, the student won't internalize new knowledge or skills. As the course moves forward, the student will find subsequent tasks to be even more difficult and confounding, creating a loop of passive compliance and answer-seeking. Productive help-seeking behavior, on the other hand, acknowledges and articulates the gap between a student's current understanding and success criteria related to a learning goal.

FIGURE 8.3 STUDENT ACTIONS WHEN NAVIGATING PRODUCTIVE STRUGGLE

Student Action	Defined as	Sounds Like	Result
Help Avoidance	Students avoid asking for help for fear of looking dumb or slowing the class down or because they don't think it will matter.	(Student's internal dialogue) "I'd ask, but everyone else gets it already and I don't want to look stupid and slow the class down."	Students avoid the risks of help-seeking but fail to develop skills, give up trying, or resort to unethical behavior.
Praise-Seeking	Students seek constant praise or affirmation that their answers are correct, what they are doing is acceptable, and the teacher believes they are competent.	Frequent, consistent iterations of "Is this right? Is this OK? Is this good?"	Students depend on constant affirmation and fear making any mistakes.
Answer-Seeking	Students want to know the correct answer in order to complete a task or earn points.	"I don't know how to do this. What is the answer?"	Students get "the answer" from the teacher or a peer or by using superficial prompts with AI tools, but don't develop new skills or understandings.
Productive Help-Seeking	Students are aware of a gap between their current skill or understanding and the learning goal or success criteria. After productive struggle, students seek assistance to clarify information or improve learning efforts.	"I know how to solve this equation using the quadratic formula. I checked my answer, and I know it is correct. But when I try to solve it using factorization, I get a different answer each time. Can I show you my approach?"	Students clarify misconceptions and build independence; they've internalized a process to successfully direct and regulate their learning.

FIGURE 8.4 ANSWER-SEEKING VS. PRODUCTIVE HELP-SEEKING REQUESTS FOR HELP

	Perception of Purpose	Perception of Current Position	Perception of Need	Request for Help from AI Tools	Results
Task-Focused Example #1	Complete the math problems and show all work.	I haven't started my assignment yet.	I need to finish this by Wednesday.	Superficial answer-seeking: "What are the answers?"	Task completed, but no new learning occurs.
Task-Focused Example #2	Read the attached history article and answer the questions.	I haven't started my assignment yet.	I need to finish this by Wednesday.	Superficial answer-seeking: "What are the answers?"	
Goal-Focused Example #1	Use precise mathematics vocabulary to explain how a linear equation can be applied to a real-world scenario.	I know how to use linear equations to solve for a value of X, but I don't know the definitions of the terms on the vocabulary list.	I'll need to review definitions of the terms and ensure I can apply the right ones in the right way in my explanations.	Productive help-seeking: "I've pasted definitions of the terms below using my own words and I've used each term in a sentence. Can you read these and provide feedback?"	Student builds agency and independence to support conditions and apply strategies for intentional learning.
Goal-Focused Example #2	Describe a variety of push and pull factors related to immigration.	I don't know what push and pull factors are.	I'll need to examine the article closely for examples of push and pull factors. If they aren't explained in the article, I'll have to learn what they are.	Productive help-seeking: "I am trying to learn the difference between push and pull factors related to immigration. Can you help check my understanding?	

Independent Learners Seek and Apply Feedback

Feedback is information about a performance that affirms or informs strategy and effort to improve. As Dylan Wiliam (2016) explains, "The only important thing about feedback is what students do with it" (p. 10). Unfortunately, out of logistical necessity, most feedback is given by the teacher to the whole class, yet it is ignored by individual students because they don't think it applies to them (Carless, 2006). Or, when individual feedback is given to students, it is often received *after* it might have been useful to inform their efforts to improve.

Independent Learners Are Persistent and Assertive

Earlier in this chapter I shared a quote from Reeve and Shin (2020) about how learners with a strong sense of agency advocate for their learning needs. Figure 8.5 provides examples of the types of needs Reeve and Shin have identified in their research, as aligned to some examples that I've adapted to show how students might advocate for those needs to be met.

Independent Learners Monitor Progress and Reflect on Results

Independent learners are willing to engage in productive struggle. However, they don't do this blindly. They seek to apply effortful strategies that are well-aligned to specific types of tasks and goals. According to research by Stephany Duany Rea and her colleagues (2022), it is not enough for students to be aware of effective strategies for learning; they need the resources to create them and the time to apply them.

Action Steps: Empower Students to Use AI Tools Intentionally

Students can use AI tools to engage in the six high-leverage skills described in the previous section. To empower students to use AI as a tool for intentional, independent learning, use the following action steps.

1. Teach students how AI tools can be used to pursue learning goals.
2. Teach students how AI tools can be used to self-assess.

FIGURE 8.5 SAMPLE EXPRESSIONS OF STUDENT AGENCY

Examples of Agency (Adapted from Reeve & Shin, 2020)	Student Language
Student lets the teacher know their interests.	"I know this is a math class, but I'm hoping I can apply some of what I learn to ceramics and pottery."
Student expresses preferences for learning.	"I've read this through twice. I think it would make more sense if I could use a graphic organizer."
Student asks pointed questions.	"I still don't get it; why are quadratic equations always shaped like that? Can you explain it another way?"
Student asks for support and guidance.	"You keep saying 'dichotomous,' but I have no idea what that means. Can you give a few examples?"
Student asks for necessary resources.	"Can you give me a few more practice problems?"

3. Teach students how to ask AI tools for help.

4. Teach students how AI tools can be used to provide meaningful feedback.

5. Teach students how to be persistent and assertive when using AI tools.

6. Teach students how AI tools can be used to apply strategies for learning.

Action Step 1: Teach Students How to Use AI Tools to Pursue Learning Goals

To support students' efforts to use AI tools in ways that support intentional learning, there are four elements that will be required for most of the prompts that will be described across each of these action steps and examples.

1. **Provide goals and success criteria:** Students will almost always need to provide the AI tool with the learning goal and success criteria.

2. **Set context:** Students will need to provide the AI tool with their context, such as "I am a 10th grader," "I am taking an Advanced Placement Chemistry course," or "I am learning about [topic] for the first time, and I am getting frustrated."

3. **Provide a role:** Students will need to provide the AI tool with a role. Examples include the following:
   - "You are a patient, supportive teacher who will work with me to . . ."
   - "You are a learning coach who will engage me in dialogue about . . ."
   - "You are a thought partner who will help me generate ideas for . . ."

4. **Provide boundaries:** State clear boundaries (these are essential to avoid the types of superficial prompts that harm learning that were described in Chapter 6) that the AI tool must follow. Examples include the following:
   - "Do not give me answers until I've attempted solutions."
   - "Don't tell me everything you know about a topic. Keep your responses short."
   - "Go slowly; go one step at a time as you guide me through this process."
   - "Before moving on, always ask me if I have any clarifying questions."

Action Step 2: Teach Students How AI Tools Can Be Used to Self-Assess

Self-assessment requires awareness of three elements: the goal, the current evidence of learning, and success criteria. Given these three elements and some frames for prompting, students can be taught to use AI tools to self-assess.

General prompt frame for students to use an AI tool to self-assess:

- **Set context:** I am a [grade level] student taking [name of class].
- **State the goal:** I am trying to learn/learn how to [learning goal].
- **Request a task to gather evidence:** I would like to take a practice assessment on [specific information or skill].
- **Provide boundaries:** Don't tell me the answers right away. Let me take the assessment first.
- **Provide criteria for quality:** Then, review my answers/responses/ evidence for [success criteria].

Sample Prompt to Self-Assess Knowledge-Level Goals

I am an 8th grade student taking an Earth science class. I am learning how to identify different types of rocks based on important characteristics. Can you give me a 12-question, multiple-choice quiz on the vocabulary terms I've pasted below? Don't give me the answers as I'd like to take the assessment first. Then, after I've replied with my answers, correct my assessment for accuracy.

Sample Prompt to Self-Assess Descriptive/Definitional Goals

I am a high school student taking a global geography class. I am learning the definitions of important terms for this unit that I've pasted below. I'd like you to help me self-assess my knowledge of each of these terms. First, ask me to write a one-sentence definition of each term. Then, ask me to give an example of how that term can be used in a meaningful sentence. After I've written the definitions and provided examples for all terms, review and correct my responses for accuracy.

Sample Prompts to Self-Assess Explanatory/ Relational Learning Goals

- I am a high school student taking an algebra course. I am supposed to be able to "explain the difference in the structure and function of linear, as compared to quadratic, equations using precise, relevant, mathematical vocabulary." Can you ask me three or four questions about the structure and function of these types of equations and then review my responses for accuracy, conceptual understanding, and precise use of academic vocabulary?

- I am a high school student taking a history course. I am supposed to be able to "compare and contrast the Articles of Confederation with the Constitution as related to the separation of powers and states' rights." I've read the introductory article my teacher provided (attached) and I think it makes sense to me. Can you ask me four open-ended questions about important differences discussed in the article? Then, after I've replied, review my responses for accuracy and clarity.

Action Step 3: Teach Students How to Use AI Tools for Productive Help

To teach students how AI tools can be used to ask for help, use the following sample prompts and sentence frames.

Sample Prompt Frame to Clarify Content or Concepts

I know that [*student writes as much detail as they can*], but I don't understand/I'm stuck on (the student selects and completes one of the following for the prompt):

- Important facts related to _____.
- The definition of _____.
- How _____ and _____ are similar.
- The difference between _____ and _____.
- Why _____.
- How the parts of _____ work.
- The cause and effect of _____.
- What happens to _____ when _____.
- Why/how _____ causes _____.
- The definition of _____.
- Examples, and non-examples of _____.
- The important attributes of _____ and how they differ from _____.

Can you help me clarify my thinking?

Sample Prompt to Clarify Why an Answer Is Incorrect

I was asked _____ and I answered _____. I know that my answer is incorrect, but I don't understand why. Can you explain why it is incorrect?

Sample Prompt to Develop a Learning Strategy

I am trying to _____, but I am not sure where to begin or what steps to take to complete that process. Can you recommend a step-by-step approach?

Sample Prompt to Clarify Next Steps

I am trying to _____. So far, I've _____, but now I am stuck. I am not sure what to do next. Can you help me understand what I am doing wrong and what I am supposed to do instead?

Action Step 4: Teach Students How AI Tools Can Be Used to Provide Meaningful Feedback

Feedback builds on the three elements of self-assessment (a description of the relationship between *the evidence* and *the goal* as related to *the success criteria*) and adds a fourth element: *What should I do to affirm or inform my next steps toward understanding*? Note, the examples below would have been preceded by a prompt that includes details about the context, learning goal, success criteria, role, and boundaries.

Sample Prompt for Feedback on Knowledge Goals

Rather than just scoring my answers as right or wrong, please provide detailed feedback. Let me know which items were correct and why. Also, let me know which items were incorrect, why my response was incorrect, and what the correct answer was and why.

Sample Prompt for Feedback on Conceptual/Relational Goals

Please provide feedback on my written explanations. The feedback should describe the strengths and accuracies of my explanations. The feedback should also describe misconceptions, inaccuracies, or weaknesses in my explanations.

Sample Prompt for Feedback About Quality of a Performance Task

> I've uploaded the success criteria for [performance task] and I've uploaded my current draft. Please provide feedback related to each element of the success criteria. The feedback should include affirmations of strengths and specific opportunities for improvement. If an element is missing or seems completely misaligned, be sure to let me know that it must be addressed.

Sample Prompt to Affirm and Inform Next Efforts

> At the end of our session, please provide me with a summary of important ideas we've reviewed, a list of content, concepts, or skills that I should continue to work on, and some specific strategies I can use to develop a deeper understanding of the content, concepts, or skills.

Action Step 5: Teach Students How to Be Persistent and Assertive When Using AI Tools

By teaching students to be persistently assertive when using AI tools, all students benefit. The rogue learners no longer need to withhold 95 percent of the questions they'd like to ask, and the wallflowers have space to exercise their agency and begin to find their voice. Here are just a few ways students can express different types of agency with AI tools.

Sample Prompts to Let the AI Tool Know Your Interests

> - I am interested in _____. Can you give an example using that topic as an analogy?
> - I know the reading is on the French Revolution and that topic is new to me. I understand a lot about the American Revolution. As we discuss the French Revolution, can you help me make relevant comparisons?

Sample Prompts to Express Preferences for Learning

> - I've answered the questions from my teacher, but I'd prefer to arrange the information using a graphic organizer. Can you help me set that up?

- I'd prefer you read one paragraph aloud to me at a time and ask me a couple of questions after each paragraph to confirm my understanding.
- Without a context for the variables in the equation, I am having a hard time visualizing what it means. Can you give a real-world context where that equation could be used?
- When you give me too much information in one response, it causes me to want to shut down. Let's try again. Only discuss one important idea at a time.
- Explain this to me like I'm in 3rd grade.
- Your explanation as to how those two things are similar wasn't very helpful to me because both of those concepts are new to me. Can you try again?
- I can see that the correct answer is the Articles of Confederation, but I still don't understand why the federal government didn't have any power. Can you explain it to me differently?
- I am still confused. What is another approach we could take?

Sample Prompts for Additional Support and Guidance

- I'm going to paraphrase what I think you are telling me in my own words. Let me know if I'm correct. Please correct any misconceptions or errors.
- Given the topic sentence, which of these paragraphs do you think is clearer and why?
- Let's take a step back. Can you provide a definition and give an example of [term or concept]?
- I am not clear on the difference between *analyze* and *synthesize*. Can you define each term and give an example based on the article I've uploaded?
- I'd like another example that isn't so complex.
- I need a brainstorming partner. What are some ways I could generate ideas/organize ideas/think about this differently?
- I'm ready to try again. Can you give me another assessment on [topic]?

Action Step 6: Teach Students How AI Tools Can Be Used to Apply Strategies for Learning

Consider the following prompts that students could use to independently pursue different types of learning goals. These prompts can be used for students to take an active role in studying for assessments, clarifying misconceptions, or engaging in distributed practice. Notice how the verbs of the learning goals can be used to clarify the type of strategy or resource that will be most helpful to the learner.

Sample Prompts for Goals or Criteria Using the Terms "Identify" or "Define"

- **For matching activities:** Can you help me create a matching activity to pair scientific terms with their definitions? I've pasted the words and their definitions below.
- **For flashcards:** Can you help me create flashcards for the key terms in my biology class?
- **For labeling diagrams:** Provide a blank diagram of the human heart for me to label the different parts. I've pasted the parts I need to identify below. Do not complete the diagram for me.
- **For mnemonic devices:** Help me create a mnemonic device to memorize the name and function of each of the 12 cranial nerves.
- **For a song rewrite:** Write song lyrics using the structure of "Yankee Doodle" to help me memorize the name and function of each of the 12 cranial nerves. There should be 12 verses and no chorus.

Sample Prompts for Goals or Criteria Using the Term "Summarize"

- **For a fiction passage:** I just read Chapter [X] in [title of novel]. Going one step at a time, ask me about significant decisions or events that established character or moved the story forward. Then, check my thinking for accuracy. Next, ask me to turn my responses into a coherent summary. Finally, give me feedback as to the accuracy and conciseness of my summary.
- **For a nonfiction passage:** I just read the attached article. Going one step at a time, ask me about the author's central argument, claims, and evidence. Then, check my thinking for accuracy. Next, ask me to turn my responses into a coherent summary. Finally, give me feedback as to the accuracy and conciseness of my summary.

Sample Prompts for Goals or Criteria Using the Terms "Compare and Contrast" or "Explain Processes, Relationships, or Events"

- **For compare and contrast:** Ask me four questions that require me to explain important differences between the Articles of Confederation and the U.S. Constitution. Then, provide feedback that affirms accurate understandings, points out any errors or misconceptions, and then coaches me to revise my work.
- **For written explanations:** Ask me to explain the process of how a bill becomes a law. Ask questions one step at a time and coach me to correct any errors or misconceptions.
- **For explaining process, relationships, or events:** Develop a 12-question, multiple-choice quiz that asks about important processes and relationships in the Krebs cycle. Responses should be labeled A through F and include "none of the above" and "some of the above." Don't provide the answers. Give me feedback about which items were wrong and why, then engage me in dialogue about each item I got wrong until I can explain the process or relationships correctly.

Sample Prompts for Goals or Criteria Using the Terms "Evaluate," "Analyze," or "Determine an Approach and Justify Your Reasoning"

- **For critical thinking questions:** Can you provide four critical thinking questions that require me to analyze how different types of governments attempt to balance individual rights and the common good? The questions should include verbs such as *explain* and *justify* and terms such as *claim*, *evidence*, and *reasoning*.
- **For debates:** I'd like to debate the following statement: "In *To Kill a Mockingbird*, Scout is a reliable narrator." I'll take the position against the claim. You take the position for the claim. You go first. After we've both taken our turn, lead me through a dialogue to continue the debate.
- **For analyzing a historical document or source:** Read the attached article. Then, ask me (don't tell me) a series of questions that require me to state the main idea and the author's. Finally, let's engage in a dialogue about my answers.

Sample Prompts for Goals or Criteria Using the Terms "Further Explain" or "What Do You Think Would Happen If . . ."

- **For open-ended questions:** Please give me some hypothetical scenarios related to [topic] that use the following format: "If instead of (cause), (alternate cause) occurred, how might the results have been different?" I'll select one of the options and reply. Then, we can engage in dialogue about my answer. My response should include specific claims, clear evidence, and logical reasoning. After I've replied, ask me questions to challenge or further my thinking.
- **For perspective-taking exercises:** Help me analyze [historical event or events in a book] by explaining those events from two different perspectives. You ask the questions and provide your answer first from the plausible perspective of [historical figure or character], then I'll answer the same question based on the plausible perspective of [another historical figure or character].
- **For Socratic seminars:** I'd like to engage in a Socratic seminar on the ethics of civil disobedience. I just finished reading Martin Luther King Jr.'s "Letter from a Birmingham Jail." Can you lead the seminar and I will respond? I will be Student 1. In addition to facilitating the seminar, I'd like you to respond as Student 2 and Student 3. The students should take turns going first. That way, they can respond to one another's comments.

Sample Prompts for Goals or Criteria Using the Term "Generating Ideas"

- **For brainstorming and narrowing exercises:** I want you to help me brainstorm some ideas for a paper I need to write about "an object that was once very important to me, but it is no longer valued by me, and it is no longer in my possession." Coach me through one question at a time so I build ownership of the ideas related to the object I finally decide on. Once we've identified several options, ask me questions to narrow my choices. Then, once I decide on an object, ask me some questions to help me recall some important details about the object.
- **For analyzing the "5 Whys":** I'd like you to help me use the "5 Whys" strategy to get at the root cause of a societal issue. The issue I am looking into is "Why don't more people use public transportation?" Don't tell me, but ask me questions and coach me. Go one step at a time. Then, summarize my responses.

Some General Guidance on These Six Action Steps

When teaching students how to prompt AI tools intentionally, keep the following in mind.

The Prompts

- Emphasize the importance of learning goals to ensure students can see beyond superficial uses of AI tools.
- Emphasize the use of very specific roles and constraints. AI tools will want to *give answers*. Remind your students that it is up to them to teach AI tools how people learn. *Slow down . . . go one step at a time.*

Gradual Release of Responsibility

- Before using these prompts in class, try them yourself to troubleshoot specifics as though you are a student.
- Teach students that different types of learning goals require different types of learning strategies. This will help them build agency to understand why different types of prompts are needed to support different types of goals or strategies.
- Take your time to help students see AI as a tool for learning. Model what you expect and give them opportunities for guided practice and play.

Connecting Back to Classroom Practice

- Use the guiding principles and reflection questions related to integrity, transparency, and explainability to support students' responsible use of these skills.
- Integrate students' uses of AI tools into classroom practice. This could include using entrance slips to find out what students learned from an AI-related task or having students take a screenshot of an exchange with an AI tool that they thought was particularly helpful.
- Have students bring their AI-generated quizzes, feedback, or other resources into class. Then use them to facilitate discussions about the content they were learning, the strategies they'd used, or the accuracies and errors of the AI tools.

Questions for Reflection and Discussion

1. What does it mean to be a dependent learner, and how does it undermine effective teaching and learning? How might AI tools exacerbate the challenge of dependence?

2. What does it mean to be an independent learner with agency, and how does it support effective teaching and learning?

3. About what percent of your students would you describe as minimalists, typically high achievers, or rogue learners? What are some implications for your teaching?

4. About what percent of your students would be more than willing to use AI tools in a task-focused versus goal-focused way? What are some implications for your teaching?

5. What are the benefits and drawbacks of a "factory model" of schooling? How does this compare to potential benefits and drawbacks of how AI tools will change schooling?

6. How do you currently use learning goals to focus your teaching? How do students use goals to focus their learning efforts?

7. Of the strategies used by independent learners discussed in this chapter, which would your students most benefit from regardless of access to AI tools? Which would your students most benefit from if applied to AI tools?

References

Acar, O. (2023, June 6). AI prompt engineering isn't the future. *Harvard Business Review*. https://hbr.org/2023/06/ai-prompt-engineering-isnt-the-future

Anderman, M., & Gray, D. L. (2017). The roles of schools and teachers in fostering competence and motivation. In A. J. Elliot, C. S. Dweck, & D. S. Yeager (Eds.), *Handbook of competence and motivation: Theory and application* (2nd ed., pp. 604–619). Guilford Press.

Anderson, L. W., & Krathwohl, D. R. (2001). *A taxonomy for learning, teaching, and assessing: A revision of Bloom's Taxonomy of educational objectives*. Longman.

Annenberg Institute at Brown University. (2022, Oct. 14). *Does tutoring work? An education economist examines the evidence on whether it's effective*. https://annenberg.brown .edu/news/does-tutoring-work-education-economist-examines-evidence-whether -its-effective.

Atkinson, J. W. (1964). *An introduction to motivation*. Van Nostrand.

Baillifard, A., Gabella, M., Lavenex, P. B., & Martarelli, C. S. (2025). Effective learning with a personal AI tutor: A case study. *Education and Information Technologies,* 297–312. https://doi.org/10.1007/s10639-024-12888-5

Bandura, A. (2006). Toward a psychology of human agency. *Perspectives on Psychological Science, 1*(2), 164–180.

Bass, D. (2023, June 23). Microsoft invests $10 billion in ChatGPT maker Open AI. *Bloomberg*. https://www.bloomberg.com/news/articles/2023-01-23/microsoft-makes-multibillion -dollar-investment-in-openai

Bastani, H., Bastani, O., Sungu, A., Ge, H., Kabakci, O., & Meraman, R. (2024). Generative AI can harm learning. *The Wharton School Research Paper*. http://dx.doi.org/10.2139 /ssrn.4895486

Bereiter C., & Scardamalia M. (1989). Intentional learning as a goal of instruction. In Resnick L. (Ed.), *Knowing, learning, and instruction: Essays in honor of Robert Glaser* (pp. 361– 392). Lawrence Erlbaum Associates, Inc.

Biggs, J. B., & Colis, K. F. (1982). *Evaluating the quality of learning: The SOLO taxonomy (structure of the observed learning outcome)*. Academic Press.

Bjelobaba, S., Foltýnek, T., Popoola, O., Šigut, P., & Waddington, L. (2023). Testing of detection tools for AI-generated text. *ArXiv*. https://doi.org/10.1007/s40979-023-00146-z

Black, P., & Wiliam, D. (1998). Inside the black box: Raising standards through classroom assessment. *Phi Delta Kappan, 80*(2), 139–148.

Brookhart., S. M. (2017). *How to give effective feedback to your students* (2nd ed.). ASCD.

Brown, P. C., Roediger III, H. L., & McDaniel, M. A. (2014). *Make it stick: The science of successful learning*. Harvard University Press.

Burgason, K., Sefiha, O., & Briggs, L. (2019). Cheating is in the eye of the beholder: An evolving understanding of academic misconduct. *Innovative Higher Education, 44*(1), 1–16.

Burns, J. M. (1978). *Leadership*. Harper & Row.

Cambridge International Teaching and Learning Team. (2019). Getting started with metacognition. https://cambridge-community.org.uk/professional-development/gswmeta/index.html

Carless, D. (2006). Differing perceptions in the feedback process. *Studies in Higher Education, 31*(2), 219–33.

Carr, N. (2008). Is Google making us stupid? *Atlantic Monthly, 302*(1), 56.

Center for Academic Integrity. https://academicintegrity.org/

Chi, M. T. H., Glaser, R., & Farr, M. J. (1988). *The nature of expertise*. Erlbaum.

Christian, B. (2020). *The alignment problem: Machine learning and human values*. Norton.

Culatta, R. (2021). *Digital for good: Raising kids to thrive in an online world*. Harvard Business Review Press.

Deci, E. L., & Ryan, R. M. (1985). *Intrinsic motivation and self-determination in human behavior*. Plenum.

Deci, E. L., & Ryan, R. M. (2017). *Self-determination theory: Basic psychological needs in motivation, development, and wellness*. Guilford Press.

Deslauriers, L. , McCarty, L. S., Miller, K., Callaghan, K., Kesin, G. (2019). Measuring actual learning versus feeling of learning in response to being actively engaged in the classroom. *PNAS, 116*(39), 19251–19257.

Doan, S., Steiner, E. D., Pandey, R., & Woo, A. (2023). Teacher well-being and intentions to leave: Findings from the 2023 State of the American Teacher survey. *RAND*. https://www.rand.org/pubs/research_reports/RRA1108-8.html

Dougall, J. (2023, July 10). Help students think more deeply with ChatGPT. *ISTE*. https://iste.org/blog/help-students-think-more-deeply-with-chatgpt

Dweck, C. S. (2006). *Mindset: The new psychology of success*. Random House.

Eccles, J. S. (1984). Sex differences in achievement patterns. In T. Sonderegger (Ed.), *Nebraska Symposium on Motivation* (Vol. 32, pp. 97–132). University of Nebraska Press.

Edmondson, A. C., & Lei, Z. (2014). Psychological safety: The history, renaissance, and future of an interpersonal construct. *Annual Review of Organizational Psychology and Organizational Behavior, 1,* 23–43.

Ericsson, K. A. (2006). The influence of experience and deliberate practice on the development of superior expert performance. In K. A. Ericsson, N. Charness, P. Feltovichm, & R. R. Hoffman (Eds.), *Cambridge handbook of expertise and expert performance* (pp. 685–706). Cambridge University Press.

Ericsson, K. A., & Poole, R. (2016). *Peak: Secrets from the new science of expertise*. Mariner Books.

Flavell, J. H. (1979). Metacognitions and cognitive monitoring: A new era of cognitive-developmental inquiry. *American Psychologist, 34,* 906–911.

Fleckenstein, J., Meyer, J., Jansen, T., Keller, S. D., Köller, O., & Möller, J. (2024). Do teachers spot AI? Evaluating the detectability of AI-generated texts among student essays. *Computers and Education: Artificial Intelligence, 6,* 100209. https://doi.org/10.1016/j.caeai.2024.100209

Frey, N., Hattie, J., & Fisher, D. (2018). *Developing assessment-capable learners, grades K–12: Maximizing skill, will, and thrill*. Corwin.

Frontier, T. (2025, February). Deeper learning, not passive compliance. *Educational Leadership, 82*(5),18–23.

Frontier, T. (2023). Taking a transformative approach to AI. *Educational Leadership, 80*(9), 12–17.

Frontier, T. (2021). *Teaching with clarity: How to prioritize and do less so students understand more*. ASCD.

Frontier, T., & Mielke, P. (2016). *Making teachers better, not bitter: Balancing evaluation, supervision, and reflection for professional growth*. ASCD.

Frontier, T., & Rickabaugh, J. (2014). *Five levers to improve learning: How to prioritize for powerful results in your school*. ASCD.

Fujita, A. (2012, March 16). GPS tracking disaster: Japanese tourists drive straight into the Pacific. *ABC News*. https://abcnews.go.com/blogs/headlines/2012/03/gps-tracking-disaster-japanese-tourists-drive-straight-into-the-pacific

Gartner. (2024). Gartner Hype Cycle. https://www.gartner.com/en/research/methodologies/gartner-hype-cycle

Gershensen, S., & Holt, S. (2022). How much do teachers struggle with stress and burnout? *Brookings*. https://www.brookings.edu/articles/how-much-do-teachers-struggle-with-stress-and-burnout/

Haidt, J. (2024). *The anxious generation: how the great rewiring of childhood is causing an epidemic of mental illness*. Penguin.

Hattie, J. (2012). *Visible learning for teachers: Maximizing impact on learning*. Routledge.

Hattie, J. 2023. *Visible learning: The sequel. A synthesis of over 2,100 meta-analyses relating to achievement*. Routledge.

Heath, C., & Heath, D. (2006). The curse of knowledge. *Harvard Business Review, 84*(12), 20–23.

Heifetz, R., & Linsky, M. (2017). *Leadership on the line: Staying alive through the dangers of change*. Harvard Business Press.

Herman, D. (2022, Dec. 9). The end of high school English. *The Atlantic*. https://www.theatlantic.com/technology/archive/2022/12/openai-chatgpt-writing-high-school-english-essay/672412/

Hunter, T. (2023, March 22). 3 things everyone's getting wrong about AI. *The Washington Post*. https://www.washingtonpost.com/technology/2023/03/22/ai-red-flags-misinformation/

Jensen L. A., Arnett, J. S., Feldman, S. S., & Cauffman, E. (2002). It's wrong, but everybody does it: Academic dishonesty among high school and college Students. *Contemporary Educational Psychology, 27*, 209–228.

Kahneman, D. (2013). *Thinking, fast and slow*. Farrar, Straus and Giroux.

Kardas, M., & O'Brien, E. (2018). Easier seen than done: Merely watching others perform can foster an illusion of skill acquisition. *Psychological Science, 29*(4), 521–536.

Kasparov, G. (2017). *Deep thinking: Where machine intelligence ends and human creativity begins*. Public Affairs.

Kestin, G., Miller, K., Klales, A., Milbourne, T., & Ponti, G. (2024). AI tutoring outperforms active learning. https://doi.org/10.21203/rs.3.rs-4243877/v1

Kumar, H., Rothschild, D. M., Goldstein, D. G., Hofman, J. M. (2023) Math education with large language models: Peril or promise? SSRN: https://dx.doi.org/10.2139/ssrn.4641653

Laflen, A., & Smith, M. (2017). Responding to student writing online: Tracking student interactions with instructor feedback in a learning management system. *Assessment Writing, 31*, 45.

Lanier, J. (2023). There is no AI: There are ways of controlling the new technology—but first we have to stop mythologizing it. *The New Yorker*. https://www.newyorker.com/science/annals-of-artificial-intelligence/there-is-no-ai

Lee, V. R., Pope, D., Miles, S., & Zárate, R. C. (2024). Cheating in the age of generative AI: A high school survey study of cheating behaviors before and after the release of ChatGPT. Computers and Education: Artificial Intelligence, v7:1-10.

Lucariello, J. (2015, March 9). *How do I get my students over their alternative conceptions (misconceptions) for learning*. American Psychological Association. https://www.apa.org/education-career/k12/misconceptions.

Maeda, J. (2006). 2 letters 2B human. *Thoughts in simplicity*. https://web.archive.org/web/20080621154444/http://weblogs.media.mit.edu/SIMPLICITY/archives/000378.html

Marzano, R. (2007). *The art & science of teaching*. ASCD.

Marzano, R. J., Frontier, T., & Livingston, D. (2011). *Effective supervision: Supporting the art & science of teaching*. ASCD.

McKeown, G. (2014). *Essentialism: The disciplined pursuit of less.* Crown.

McQuade, B. (2024). *Attacked from within: How disinformation is sabotaging America.* Seven Stories.

McTighe, J., & Silver, H. F. (2020). *Teaching for deeper learning: Tools to engage students in meaning making.* ASCD.

McTighe, J., & Frontier, T. (2022). How to provide better feedback through rubrics. *Educational Leadership, 79*(7), 17–23.

Meckler, L., & Verma, P. (2022, Dec. 28). Teachers are on alert for inevitable cheating after release of ChatGPT. *The Washington Post.* https://www.washingtonpost.com/education /2022/12/28/chatbot-cheating-ai-chatbotgpt-teachers/

Metcalfe, J. (2017). Learning from errors. *The Annual Review of Psychology, 68*, 465–489.

Meyer, H., Haywood, N., Sachdev, D., & Faraday, S. (2008). *Independent learning: Literature Review.* Learning and Skills Network.

Mitchell, M. (2019). *Artificial intelligence: A guide for thinking humans.* Pelican Books.

Moeller, J., Brackett, M. A., Ivcevic, Z., & White, A. E. (2020). High school students' feelings: Discoveries from a large national survey and an experience sampling study. *Learning and Instruction, 66.* Article 101301. https://doi.org/10.1016/j.learninstruc.2019.101301

Mollick, E. (2025, January 25). Which AI to use now: An updated opinionated guide. *One Useful Thing.* https://www.oneusefulthing.org/p/which-ai-to-use-now-an-updated -opinionated/

Ng, A. (2023, August 29). *Opportunities in AI* [Video]. YouTube. https://youtube/5p248 yoa3oE?si=UeLrzBu5KpheNBUz

Office of the Surgeon General. (2023). Social media and youth mental health: The U.S. surgeon general's advisory. U.S. Department of Health and Human Services. http://surgeon general.gov

Ong, I. (2020). Play and flow: Harnessing flow through the power of play in adult learning. In C. Koh (Ed.), *Diversifying learner experience* (pp. 137–155). Springer. https://doi .org/10.1007/978-981-15-9861-6_8

OpenAI. (2023). New AI classifier for indicating AI-written text. https://openai.com/blog /new-ai-classifier-for-indicating-ai-written-text

Peeters, A. (2021). *Reframing errors in high school mathematics classrooms: An action science approach.* University of Auckland.

Pope, D. C. (2001) *Doing school: How we are creating a generation of stressed out, materialistic, and miseducated students.* Yale University Press.

Pope, D., & Schrader, D. (2023, Feb. 14). We can add ChatGPT to the latest list of concerns about student cheating, but let's go deeper. *Challenge Success.* https://challengesuccess. org/resources/opinion-we-can-add-chatgpt-to-the-latest-list-of-concerns-about -student-cheating-but-lets-go-deeper/

Rea, S. D., Wang, L., Muenks, K., & Yan, V. X. (2022). Students can (mostly) recognize effective learning, so why do they not do it? *Journal of Intelligence, 10*(4), 127.

Reeve, J., & Cheon, S. H. (2021). Autonomy-supportive teaching: its malleability, benefits, and potential to improve educational practice. *Educational Psychology, 56*(1), 54–77.

Reeve, J., & Shin, S. H. (2020). How teachers can support students' agentic engagement, *Theory Into Practice, 59*(2), 150–161.

Reeve, J., & Tseng, C. (2011). Agency as a fourth aspect of students' engagement during learning activities. *Contemporary Educational Psychology* 36, 257–267

Robinson, C. D., Bisht, B., & Loeb, S. (2021). The inequity of opt-in educational resources and an intervention to increase equitable access. *EdWorkingPapers.com.* https://edworking papers.com/ai22-654

Rozenblit, L., & Keil, F. (2002). The misunderstood limits of fold science: An illusion of explanatory depth. *Cognitive Science, 26*(5), 521–562.

Ryan, R. M., & Deci, E. L. (2000). Self-determination theory and the facilitation of intrinsic motivation, social development, and well-being. *American Psychologist, 55*(1), 68–78.

Schlecty, P. (2002). *Working on the work: An action plan for teachers, principals, and superintendents*. Jossey-Bass.

Senge, P. M. (2006). *The fifth discipline: The art and practice of the learning organization*. Broadway Business.

Shirky, C. (2008). *Here comes everybody: The power of organizing without organizations*. Penguin.

Simon, H. A. (1971). Designing organizations for an information-rich world. In M. Greenberger (Ed.), *Computers, communications, and the public interest* (pp. 38–72). The Johns Hopkins University Press.

Terry, O. K. (2023, May 12). I'm a student. You have no idea how much we're using ChatGPT. *The Chronicle of Higher Education*. https://www.chronicle.com/article/im-a-student -you-have-no-idea-how-much-were-using-chatgpt

Vaswani, A., Shazeer, N., Parmar, N., Uszkoreit, J., Jones, L., Gomez, A. N., Kaiser, L., & Polosukhin, I. (2017). *Attention is all you need*. https://arxiv.org/pdf/1706.03762

Wigfield, A., & Eccles, J. S. (2000). Expectancy-value theory of achievement motivation. *Contemporary Educational Psychology, 25*(1), 68–81.

Wiggins, G. P., & McTighe, J. (2005). *Understanding by design* (Expanded 2nd ed.). ASCD.

Wiliam, D. (2016). The secret of effective feedback. *Educational Leadership, 73*(7), 10–15.

Winstone, N., Bourne, J., Medland, E., Niculescu, I., & Rees, R. (2020). "Check the grade, log out": Students' engagement with feedback in learning management systems. *Assessment & Evaluation in Higher Education, 46*(4), 631–643.

Wolfram, S. (2023). *What is ChatGPT doing . . . and why does it work?* Wolfram Media.

Zhai, C., Wibowo, S., & Li, L.D. (2024). The effects of over-reliance on AI dialogue systems on students' cognitive abilities: A systematic review. *Smart Learning Environments, 11*(28).

Index

The letter *f* following a page locator denotes a figure.

fidelity before efficiency, action steps
(*continued*)
   ensure fidelity, transparency, and
      explainability of resources, 56–58
   use AI tools intentionally, 56
fidelity coach, using AI as a, 103–106
foundational model, defined, 18
frontier model, defined, 18

Gartner Hype Cycle, 19–21
generative AI, defined, 18
germane load, 73

hallucination, defined, 18
helplessness, learned, 68, 69
help-seeking
   AI tools for productive, 124–125
   answer-seeking vs. productive, 118–119,
      120*f*
humanism, behaviorism vs., 37–41
humanist, technologist vs., 31
Hype Cycle, 19–21

illusion
   of skill acquisition, 65–66, 69
   of understanding, 65, 69
innovation, predicting response to, 19–21
integrity. *See also* academic integrity
   behaviorist vs. humanist, 37–41
   defined, 45
   emphasizing the importance of, 89
   prompts for students to demonstrate, 45
intention
   guiding principles for leaders using AI
      with, 5*f*
   guiding principles for teachers using AI
      with, 6*f*
   in learning, 3, 127–130
   teaching with, 3, 32
   in use of tools, 56
   using AI tools with, 56
   using AI with, 3–4, 5–6*f*
intention, guiding principles for leadership
   using AI with. *See also specific principles*
   emphasize integrity, 36–46
   fidelity before efficiency, 47–58
   lead by learning, 9–21
   overview, 5*f*
   take a transformational approach,
      22–35
intention, guiding principles for teachers
   using AI with. *See also specific principles*
   know your purpose, 75–89
   overview, 6*f*

intention, guiding principles for teachers
   using AI with (*continued*)
   prompt AI tools intentionally, 91–110
   stand in their shoes, 61–74
   use AI tools for intentional learning,
      111–131
interest inventories, 72
internet, benefits and costs, 2
interpretability, defined, 18
intrinsic load, 73–74

jargon, learning the, 17–19

knowledge, the curse of, 62–63
know your purpose, action steps
   acknowledge superficial uses of AI can
      harm learning, 79–80
   avoid the twin sins of curriculum design,
      80–84
   emphasize integrity, transparency,
      explainability, 89
   emphasize purpose of school is for
      learning, not compliance, 84–87
   teach how to plan, monitor, and self-
      assess, 87–88, 88*f*, 89

language of rigor, 85
large language models (LLMs), 11, 18
lead by learning, action steps
   acknowledge misconceptions, 11–13
   develop a basic understanding, 10–11, 12*f*
   identify trends and patterns, 13–17
   know the Gartner Hype Cycle, 19–21
   learn the jargon, 17–19
leadership
   aligning behaviors to the magnitude of
      change, 25–29
   effective, 22, 23
   in learning vs. reactive organizations,
      9–10
   transactional vs. transformational, 23,
      24*f*, 25
leadership, guiding principles for using AI
   with intention. *See also specific principles*
   emphasize integrity, 36–46
   fidelity before efficiency, 47–58
   lead by learning, 9–21
   overview, 5*f*
   take a transformational approach,
      22–35
learn, opportunity to, 48
learners
   agentic, 113–114
   compliant, task focused, 118*f*

About the Author

 **Tony Frontier**, PhD, is an award-winning educator who works with teachers and school leaders nationally and internationally to help them prioritize efforts to improve student learning. With expertise in student engagement, evidence-based assessment, effective instruction, technology integration, data analysis, and strategic planning, Frontier emphasizes a systems approach to build capacity and empower teachers to improve each student's schooling experience.

Frontier is the author of *Teaching with Clarity: How to Prioritize and Do Less So Students Understand More* and co-author of the ASCD books *Five Levers to Improve Learning: How to Prioritize for Powerful Results in Your School* with James Rickabaugh; *Effective Supervision: Supporting the Art and Science of Teaching* with Robert J. Marzano and David Livingston; and *Making Teachers Better, Not Bitter: Balancing Evaluation, Supervision, and Reflection for Professional Growth* with Paul Mielke. He is also co-author of *Creating Passionate Learners: Engaging Today's Students for Tomorrow's World* with Kim Brown and Donald J. Viegut (Corwin). Frontier is a frequent contributor to ASCD's *Educational Leadership*, and his books have been translated and published in Korean, Mandarin, and Arabic.

In addition to his work as an author and a consultant, Frontier served as a professor of doctoral leadership studies at Cardinal Stritch University in Milwaukee, Wisconsin, where he taught courses in curriculum development, organizational learning, research methods, and statistics. As a former classroom teacher in Milwaukee Public Schools, an associate high school principal, and the director of curriculum and instruction for the Whitefish Bay School

District, Frontier brings a wealth of experience as a classroom teacher, building administrator, and central office administrator to his workshops, writing, and research.

He is available for consulting, research, and keynote presentations independently and through McTighe & Associates. He can be reached at tonyfrontier @gmail.com or through his website at tonyfrontier.com.

Related ASCD Resources

At the time of publication, the following resources were available (ASCD stock numbers in parentheses).

The AI Assist: Strategies for Integrating AI into the Very Human Act of Teaching by Nathan Lang-Raad (#124030)

Before You Say a Word: A School Leader's Guide to Clear and Compelling Communication by Erik Palmer (#124026)

EdTech Essentials: 12 Strategies for Every Classroom in the Age of AI, 2nd Edition by Monica Burns (#124028)

Five Levers to Improve Learning: How to Prioritize for Powerful Results in Your School by Tony Frontier and James Rickabaugh (#114002)

Making Teachers Better, Not Bitter: Balancing Evaluation, Supervision, and Reflection for Professional Growth by Tony Frontier and Paul Mielke (#116002)

Teaching with Clarity: How to Prioritize and Do Less So Students Understand More by Tony Frontier (#121015)

Unleashing Teacher Leadership: A Toolkit for Ensuring Effective Instruction in Every Classroom by Joshua H. Barnett (#123031)

Using AI Chatbots to Enhance Planning and Instruction (Quick Reference Guide) by Monica Burns (#QRG123066)

For up-to-date information about ASCD resources, go to www.ascd.org. You can search the complete archives of *Educational Leadership* at www.ascd.org/el. To contact us, send an email to member@ascd.org or call 1-800-933-2723 or 703-578-9600.

iste+ascd

Transform Instruction to
Transform Students' Lives

Our Transformational Learning Principles (TLPs) are evidence-based practices that ensure students have access to high-impact, joyful learning experiences.

Endorsed by AASA and NASSP, the TLPs provide a shared language and a framework for reimagining teaching and learning, focusing on nurturing student growth, guiding intellectual curiosity, and empowering learners to take ownership of their education.

AI with Intention relates to the **connect learning to the learner** and **ignite agency** principles.

Learn more at **ascd.org/tlps**